699 Ways To Improve The Performance Of Your Car

Harry Alexandrowicz

with illustrations by Robert Brashear

Sterling Publishing Co., Inc. New York
Oak Tree Press Co., Ltd. London & Sydney

NOTE

To convert miles to kilometers, simply multiply by 1.6. For example, 50 miles per hour is equal to 80 kilometers per hour.

Library of Congress Cataloging in Publication Data
Alexandrowicz, Harry.
   699 ways to improve the performance of your car.

   Includes index.
   1. Automobiles—Maintenance and repair—Amateurs'
manuals. I. Title.
TL152.A2735   629.28'722   79-93251
ISBN 0-8069-5550-3
ISBN 0-8069-5551-1 (lib. bdg.)
ISBN 0-8069-8900-9 (pbk.)
Oak Tree ISBN 7061-2702-1

Copyright © 1980 by Harry Alexandrowicz
Published by Sterling Publishing Co., Inc.
Two Park Avenue, New York, N.Y. 10016
Distributed in Australia by Oak Tree Press Co., Ltd.,
P.O. Box J34, Brickfield Hill, Sydney 2000, N.S.W.
Distributed in the United Kingdom by Ward Lock Ltd.
116 Baker Street, London W.1
Manufactured in the United States of America

CONTENTS

INTRODUCTION

The night of Easter Sunday, 1973, my wife and I were driving home on a dark country road. The car was loaded to the brim with luggage, gifts, our dog and the assorted paraphernalia that married couples always seem to be carrying around. All of a sudden the car lost power, the lights went dim, and the little red "ALT" light glared at us in all its intensity. We had not seen an open gas station for miles. I pulled the car off the side of the road. What was wrong?

If I had been prepared I would have been able to diagnose the problem, temporarily fix the car and avoid a great deal of danger and aggravation. Instead I found myself leaving my wife and child locked in the car, hitchhiking down the dark road in hopes of finding some help, eventually rousing friends out of bed to come pick us up, and paying a grumbling tow truck operator to haul my car to his station. The next day I had to bother another friend to drive me back to the station to pick up my car and pay the mechanic for the replacement of a broken fan belt. It was a costly, irritating experience, to say the least.

On January 26, 1979, I received a phone call at work. My wife was calling to say that she thought she was in labor. I quickly drove home, picked her up and drove to the doctor's office. He confirmed her feelings and told us to head for the hospital immediately. In the parking lot I turned the key in the ignition and . . . nothing. I jumped out of the car, opened the trunk, grabbed my pliers, opened the hood, squeezed the battery terminal, jumped back into the driver's seat, turned the key and drove off to the hospital. Our daughter was born 90 minutes later.

What had happened between 1973 and 1979? Well, for one thing I had decided on that Easter Sunday night that I was not going to place myself and my family at the mercy of my automobile again. I decided to educate myself on the operation and maintenance of my car.

In the process of gaining my education I found that books on the subject of auto repair were difficult to follow. It seemed like mechanics were writing for other mechanics, using vocabulary that, as a layman, I did not understand. I felt that there was a need to write a simple, easy-to-read book that you, the average person with limited or no mechanical training, could use.

One benefit of my education has been the amount of money I've saved on auto repairs. As a middle-class, white-collar worker, I've felt the crunch of inflation and have had to find ways of cutting the budget and saving money. Here was one area to accomplish such a goal. I estimate that I save approximately one to two weeks salary annually by performing the routine maintenance on my car. You can do the same if you follow the material in this book.

This book is an attempt to help you over the hurdles of car ownership. It is by no means an attempt to turn you into a master mechanic—nor is it written for master mechanics—but the information and knowledge you gain can become invaluable the next time your car breaks down or needs repairs.

Chapter One

BASIC OPERATION

Fig. 1. The carburetor.

Most of us slide behind the wheel of our car, turn the key and expect the car to start right up. Most of the time it does, so that we just take it for granted. When, however, it does not start, or it breaks down, our ignorance of how a car works comes to haunt us. By understanding what happens, or is supposed to happen, when we turn the key and step on the accelerator, we have a leg up on figuring out what went wrong and why, and a good chance of avoiding needless expenses.

A word about what you'll find in this section. In most books the glossary, if there is one, is placed at the back of the book to be used as you would use a dictionary. This book is different; here the glossary is part of the appropriate text so that you can learn what, for example, a carburetor is, while at the same time understanding how it relates to the other parts of the engine.

At the end of the book a simplified index is provided to enable you to quickly locate a particular entry in the glossary, or a specific mechanical procedure. Some terms are mentioned only in the glossary and are presented for the reader who is in need of any repairs that are beyond the scope of this book. You are urged to study the glossary entries with care so that you'll be able to at least hold your own in discussing particulars with a mechanic. Knowledge makes you a better prepared consumer and helps prevent you from being one of the millions of consumers victimized each year by unscrupulous car dealers and mechanics.

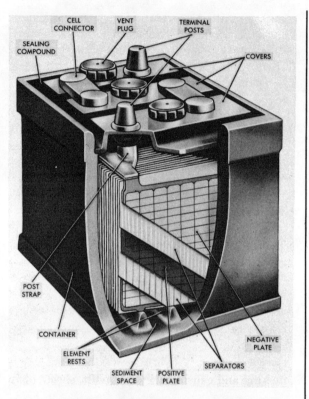

Fig. 2. Storage battery with case partially cut away to show cell construction.

The Ignition System

battery—The device that stores the electrical power demanded by the electrical system.

battery cables—The thick wires that carry the elec-

trical power from the battery to the necessary components of the engine.

battery posts—The connections that the battery cables are attached to. Also referred to as *battery terminals*.

breaker arm—The movable part of the ignition point assembly that holds one of the contact points.

cell—One of the compartments of the battery in which chemical energy is converted into electrical energy.

coil—The device that increases the battery voltage to the level necessary to fire the spark plugs.

condenser—The device in the distributor that ab-

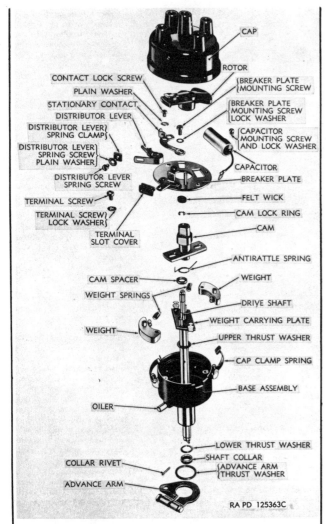

CAP
ROTOR
CONTACT LOCK SCREW
BREAKER PLATE MOUNTING SCREW
PLAIN WASHER
STATIONARY CONTACT
BREAKER PLATE MOUNTING SCREW LOCK WASHER
DISTRIBUTOR LEVER
DISTRIBUTOR LEVER SPRING CLAMP
CAPACITOR MOUNTING SCREW AND LOCK WASHER
DISTRIBUTOR LEVER SPRING SCREW PLAIN WASHER
CAPACITOR
DISTRIBUTOR LEVER SPRING SCREW
BREAKER PLATE
TERMINAL SCREW
FELT WICK
TERMINAL SCREW LOCK WASHER
CAM LOCK RING
TERMINAL SLOT COVER
CAM
ANTIRATTLE SPRING
CAM SPACER
WEIGHT
WEIGHT SPRINGS
DRIVE SHAFT
WEIGHT CARRYING PLATE
WEIGHT
UPPER THRUST WASHER
CAP CLAMP SPRING
BASE ASSEMBLY
OILER
LOWER THRUST WASHER
SHAFT COLLAR
COLLAR RIVET
ADVANCE ARM THRUST WASHER
ADVANCE ARM
RA PD 125363C

Fig. 3. The distributor—a disassembled view.

sorbs surges of electrical energy and prevents burning and arcing of the points.

distributor—The device that controls the high voltage electrical current and directs it to the spark plugs in the correct firing order.

distributor cap—The top portion of the distributor that houses the ends of the spark plug wires and through which the connection is made between the coil and the ignition points.

electrolyte—The battery fluid.

electronic ignition—Uses transistors in place of conventional breaker points and condensers.

firing order—The sequence in which the spark plugs ignite the fuel/air mixture.

ignition system—The components in the engine that combine to create the spark in the combustion chamber. The major components include the battery, distributor, points, condenser, rotor, spark plugs, spark plug wires and coil. See Fig. 4.

points—The set of electrical contacts within the distributor that produce the surge of electricity delivered to the spark plug.

rotor—The part of the distributor that revolves to sequentially direct electrical current to the spark plugs from the coil. (Also may be the disc that the brake pads press against when the brakes are applied in disc-brake systems.)

solenoid—An electromagnetic switching device. Usually it's the device that "kicks in" the starter when the ignition is turned on.

spark plug—The component in the ignition system that delivers the electrical charge to ignite the air/gas mixture in the combustion chamber.

timing—The adjustment of the ignition system to permit the firing of the spark plugs at the proper instant.

timing light—A high-intensity light that glows when the spark plug it is connected to fires. Used in setting the correct timing of the engine.

When you turn the key in your *ignition switch*, you are starting a series of events that, if all goes well, will result in your car starting and you eventually arriving at your destination. First, you are creating an electrical connection that draws power stored in the *battery*. This power goes through the system, increasing in *voltage* from 12 to 20,000 as it goes through the *coil*. Two circuits connect the coil with the *distributor*: the *primary*, or original, circuit, and the *secondary* circuit, which is of much higher voltage. The secondary circuit is activated only when the primary is shut off and is needed only to ignite the *spark plugs*. Both the activation of the secondary circuit and its distribution to the spark plugs at the right time and sequence are accomplished by the *distributor*.

The distributor (Fig. 3) is composed of the *breaker points* (usually just "points"), which is the switch that connects and disconnects the primary circuit and thereby activates the secondary current;

the *condenser*, which absorbs any excess current and facilitates the opening and closing of the points; the *cam*, which is connected to the engine camshaft and separates the points; the *rotor*, which is also driven by the camshaft and spins, making electrical contact with the *ignition wires in the distributor cap*. It is the rotor that receives the high voltage from the coil and distributes it to the spark plugs via the ignition wires.

While all this is taking place, power goes through the *starter* and the *solenoid* located on the starter. The starter is a simple electric motor that engages the ring gear that fits around the *flywheel*. The solenoid attracts current to itself and redirects it to the starter, helping the starter turn fast enough to

start the engine. This requires an enormous amount of energy from the battery—especially in cold weather—for the starter will crank the engine until it starts. The starter turns the crankshaft and thereby gets the pistons moving until the engine is able to run by itself. Once the engine is running, a belt drives the *alternator*, which provides electrical power to keep the engine running and at the same time replaces the power drained from the battery.

If your car has an *electronic ignition system*, the distributor is replaced by an electronic module that performs the operations of the points, condenser, and rotor. It is more efficient and requires less maintenance than the conventional system.

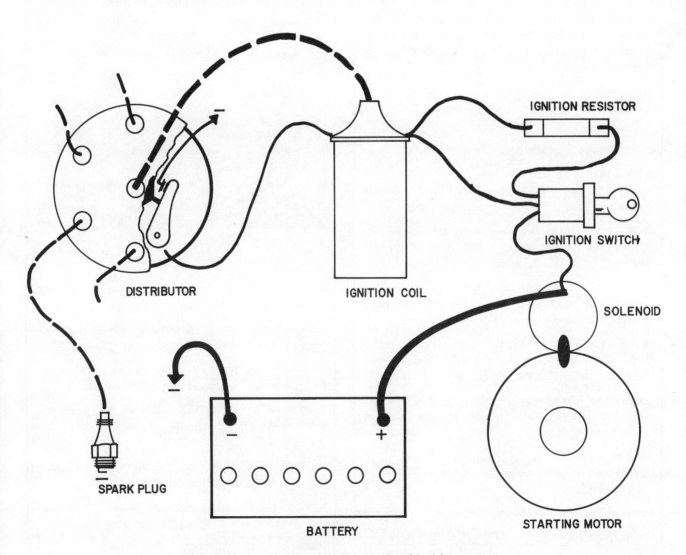

Fig. 4. The components of a conventional ignition system.

The Fuel System

accelerator pump—Small pump that injects extra gasoline into the carburetor when the accelerator pedal is depressed quickly. It produces a richer mixture and extra power to accelerate the car quickly.

additives—Chemicals added to oil or gasoline to improve performance. An example would be an additive that increases the viscosity (thickness) of oil or a gasoline additive that cleans the carburetor as the car operates.

air filter—The filter that usually fits over the carburetor to remove impurities from the air and keep the carburetor clean.

air/fuel ratio—The amount of air mixed with the gasoline to provide the most efficient combustible mixture. Approximately fifteen parts air to 1 part fuel.

air injection—An anti-pollution system that mixes air with exhaust gases to burn off unused fuel.

carbon—A combustion by-product that may collect on various parts of the engine.

carbon monoxide—A toxic gas formed by gasoline combustion. It is tasteless, odorless and colorless and can be fatal if inhaled in too great a quantity.

carburetor—The device that mixes air and fuel to provide the proper mixture for combustion and delivers it to the intake manifold.

catalytic converter—An anti-pollution device that uses chemical reactions to prevent harmful gases from reaching the atmosphere.

choke—The part of the carburetor that restricts the intake of air to provide a richer mixture of air and fuel to aid in starting the engine.

combustion chamber—The area of the cylinder where compression and ignition of the air/fuel mixture takes place.

compression—The act of reducing the volume of the air/fuel mixture by increasing the pressure in the cylinder.

compression test—The measurement of the amount of compression within the cylinder. Low readings can be indicative of valve, piston ring or combustion chamber sealing problems.

Figs. 5 and 6. You'll find the air filter and carburetor under the pan-shaped cover pictured above. Simply unscrew the butterfly nut (wing nut) and lift the cover off.

detonation—Commonly known as "knock." Results from the uneven mixture of air and gas.

dieseling—The condition in which the engine continues to run after the ignition has been turned off.

float—The hollow bulb inside the float bowl of the carburetor that operates the *needle valve*.

flooding—The phenomenon that occurs when too much gas in the carburetor prevents the car from starting.

fuel line—The hollow pipe through which fuel travels from the fuel tank to the carburetor.

fuel pump—The component that pulls the fuel from the fuel tank and pushes it to the carburetor.

idle screw—The adjustment screw of the carburetor that regulates the engine speed (rpm).

intake manifold—The pipes that connect the carburetor to the intake valves of the combustion chambers.

knock—A pinging sound that results from low octane gasoline igniting before the spark plugs fire. (See also *detonation*.)

lead-free—Gasoline that does not include lead in its chemical make-up. Late model cars that have catalytic converters as anti-pollution devices require the use of lead-free gasoline. (Also called *unleaded* or *no-lead* gasoline.)

lean mixture—An air/fuel mixture that contains a higher proportion of air than is usually required for optimum performance.

manual choke—A method of operating the butterfly valve in the carburetor by way of a cable being pushed and pulled by the driver. Most new cars have automatic chokes.

misfire—The phenomenon that occurs when the spark plugs do not fire properly. If the timing is not adjusted correctly, the result is misfiring plugs, inefficient combustion and stalling.

needle valve—Controls the amount of gasoline that enters the bowl of the carburetor. Acts much like the float in a modern toilet.

piston—The tightly fitted cylindrical piece of metal that slides up and down within the cylinder. It is attached to the crankshaft and turns the shaft as it operates. It is moved by the expansion of the burning gas/air mixture.

power stroke—The third cycle of the four-cycle engine when the piston is being driven downward after the spark plug has ignited the air/gas mixture.

preignition—Sometimes called "run on." The engine continues to operate even after the ignition is turned off. Develops as a result of hot spots in the combustion chamber.

rich mixture—An air/gas mixture containing a higher proportion of gasoline than usually required for optimum performance.

stroke—The distance that the piston moves up or down the cylinder.

vapor lock—A condition that develops when the gasoline in the fuel line boils (vaporizes) and prevents the flow of gasoline to the carburetor.

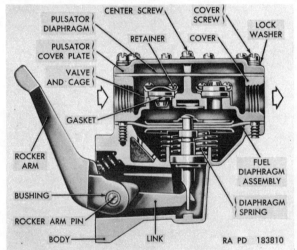

Fig. 7. The fuel pump—a sectional view.

OCTANE RATING

There are different gradations of gasoline on the market. The differences in fuel are reflected in the octane rating of the fuel. The more "anti-knock" components in the gasoline mixture, the higher the octane rating. The rating is a scale that indicates the resistance of the fuel to knock (a clicking sound upon acceleration coming from the area of the carburetor).

The driver of an older model car has more choices in the grade of gasoline he can use in his car. He is able to select from premium, leaded regular, low-lead, or no-lead. Newer models (1974 to present) must use no-lead gasoline because of the catalytic converters that are employed to reduce pollution. These cars are fitted with special fuel tank openings that will not permit the introduction of leaded fuels.

If you own an older model you can possibly save some money in buying fuel. Try a tankful of regular gas. If the car knocks move up to the next highest grade. Once you have found a fuel that does not knock, you should use that fuel.

The lead in the regular mixture is an important additive if your car is designed to use leaded fuel (check your owner's manual or call a dealer). Using no-lead gasoline in such a car robs the valves and valve seats of the necessary lubrication that is provided by the lead and can lead to damage.

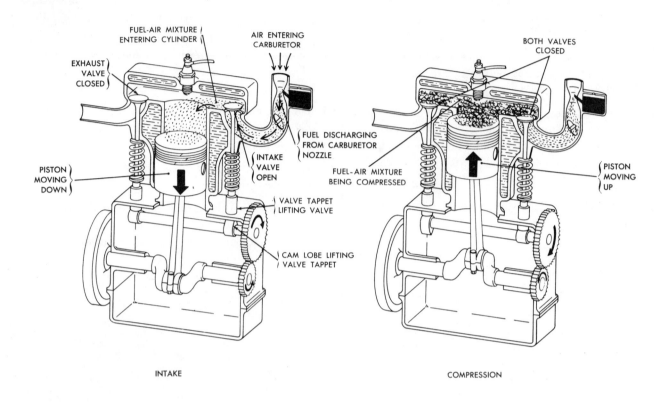

INTAKE

COMPRESSION

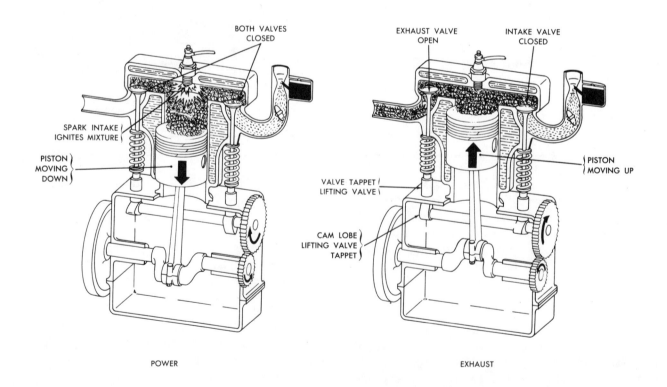

POWER

EXHAUST

Fig. 8. The four strokes in the 4-stroke cycle, gasoline engine.

As you turn the key and start the car, you also press down on the accelerator pedal and initiate another series of events. As the crankshaft begins to turn it moves a lever in the *fuel pump* which, in turn, moves a diaphragm up and down, creating a suction in the *fuel line*. This suction draws the gasoline from the *gas tank* to the *carburetor* where it is mixed with the proper proportion of air. As you step on the accelerator, the *throttle valve* in the carburetor opens and gasoline flows into the *float chamber*. In the meantime, air is drawn into the engine by the action of the pistons in the cylinders. It passes through the *air filter*, which is that disc-like object located directly above the carburetor. As the air rushes through the carburetor, it sucks gasoline into its stream and a combustible mist is formed. This mist continues through the *intake manifold* and into the cylinder through the *intake valve*.

In the *cylinder*, ignition and fuel systems meet. The high voltage created in the coil and sent to the spark plugs by the actions of the distributor meets the combustible mix from the carburetor. The electrical surge leaps across a gap on the spark plug creating the spark necessary to ignite the gas/air mixture. These explosions occur in one cylinder after another, very, very quickly and with precise timing.

Now let's see what happens in each cylinder as the engine runs. Remember that the cylinders are the spaces in which the pistons move up and down. The action of the pistons can be divided into four phases or *strokes* (see Fig. 8):

1. **Intake stroke**—The piston is near the bottom of its movement, the intake valve opens and the gas/air mixture enters from the carburetor.

2. **Compression stroke**—The intake valve closes and the piston continues upward, forcing the gas/air mixture into a smaller amount of space.

3. **Power stroke**—The piston reaches the top of its movement, the spark plug fires, igniting the gas/air mixture and thereby forcing the piston back down the cylinder.

4. **Exhaust stroke**—The piston starts up the cylinder again, the *exhaust valve* opens to let the waste gases (by-products of gasoline combustion) escape from the cylinder and into the *exhaust system*. The cylinder is now ready for a new intake stroke and the cycle begins again.

The spark must ignite the gas/air mixture at the right time or much of the energy created by the burning of the mixture is wasted. If the spark arrives too early, the piston will still be on its way up the cylinder; in either case, the force of the ignition is dissipated and your fuel economy and the performance of your car suffer. That's why timing your engine is an important procedure and something you can do to save money (see page 90).

If you own a six-cylinder car, the cycle happens six times in six different cylinders (and eight times in an eight-cylinder car) before the original piston gets stroked again. They all take their turns in the proper order.

Once the ignition system and the fuel system have completed their jobs the engine is virtually on its own. Actually, the engine helps reset the ignition system by recharging the battery as the motor runs. This is where your *alternator belt* becomes very important. Maintaining the proper tension on the belt that operates the alternator or generator is imperative.

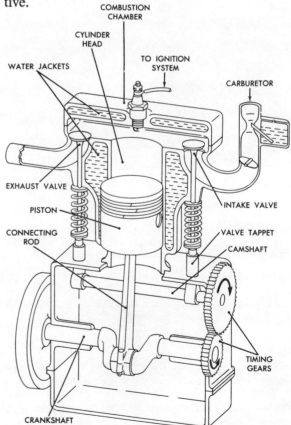

Fig. 9. Cutaway view of one cylinder of a 4-stroke cycle, internal combustion, gasoline engine.

Transmission and Driveline

ATF—Automatic Transmission Fluid. Lightweight oily fluid used to lubricate and cool automatic transmissions. Also used in some power steering systems.

automatic transmission—A transmission that changes gears without the manual operation of the clutch by the driver.

clutch—The coupling device that engages or disengages one moving part from another, such as the clutch that connects the engine to the transmission.

differential—The gear unit in the rear axle that permits the outside wheel to turn faster than the inside wheel during a turn.

driveshaft—The long shaft under the car between the transmission and the differential. The driveshaft transfers power from the transmission to the differential.

flywheel—A large disc attached to the crankshaft designed to smooth out the operation of the engine.

pressure plate—The part of the clutch that rubs against the flywheel of the engine, allowing the engine to connect with the transmission.

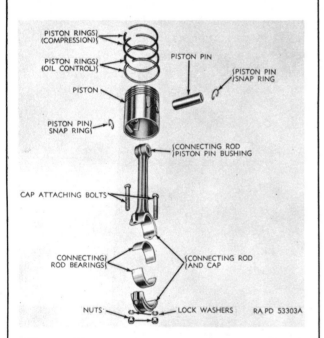

Fig. 10. Piston, piston rings, connecting rod, and connecting rod bearings.

connecting rods—The rigid metal shafts that form the link between the pistons and the crankshaft.

crankcase—The lower portion of the engine that houses the crankshaft.

crankshaft—The major part of the engine driven by the pistons and connecting rods.

Okay, you've turned the key, stepped on the accelerator and the pistons are now moving up and down in the cylinders. The next order of business is to get the car moving.

The pistons are attached to the crankshaft by the *connecting rods* (Fig. 10), and the turning of the crankshaft transfers the motion of the pistons to the *driveshaft* by means of the *transmission*. The transmission is a complex mechanism composed of two sets of *gears*, one coming from the crankshaft, the other connected to the driveshaft. The relationship of the two sets of gears translates engine speed into the appropriate driveshaft speed—appropriate, that is, for your driving situation, so that you move in the most efficient manner.

In low gear, the high speed of the engine is transformed into a low turning speed of the driveshaft so that you have the power necessary to begin to move. Here the crankshaft turns 2¼ times for each turn of the driveshaft. In second gear, less power and more speed is required and the crankshaft only turns 1½ times for each turn of the driveshaft. In high gear the speed of the crankshaft is the same as that of the driveshaft.

The driveshaft is the long pipe that extends from the transmission to the *differential* where, by another set of gears, the power changes direction and goes sideways to the rear wheels. The differential is a large, ball-like component that allows one of the rear wheels to spin faster than the other when you make a turn or are traveling in anything but a straight line.

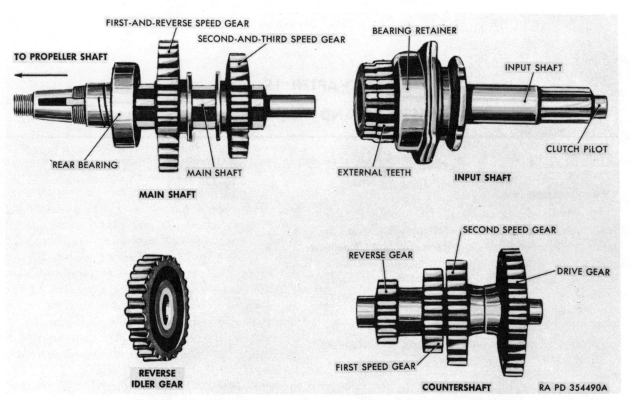

Fig. 11. The principal gear groups of a 3-speed transmission system.

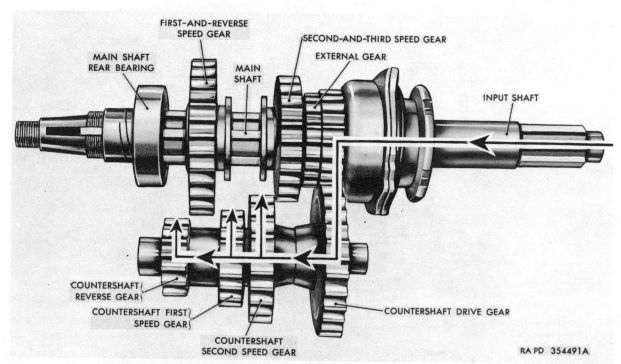

Fig. 12. Transmission gears in neutral position.

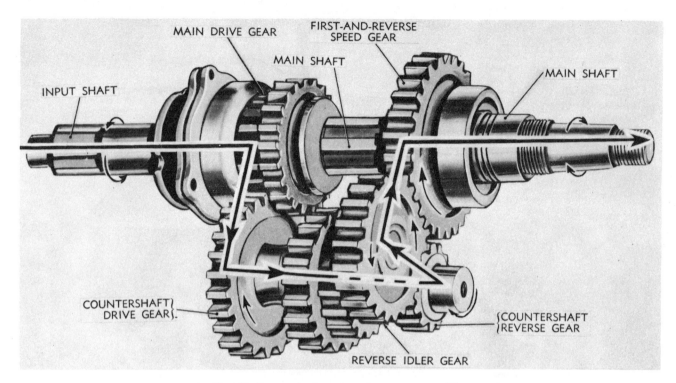

Fig. 13. Transmission gears in reverse position.

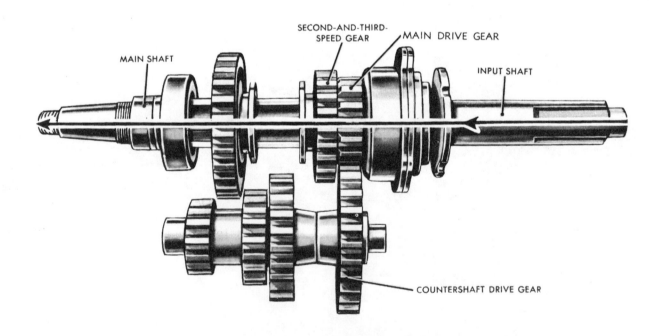

Fig. 14. Transmission gears in third-speed or direct-drive position.

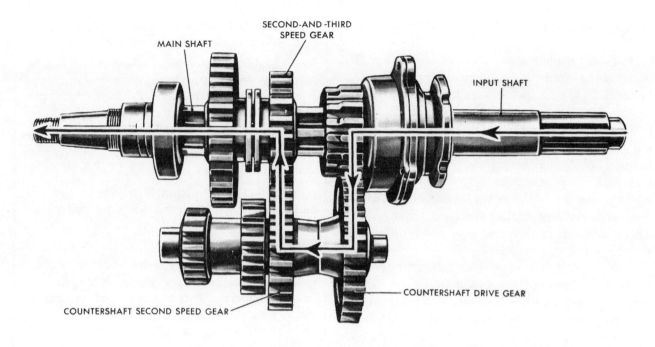

MAIN SHAFT

SECOND-AND-THIRD SPEED GEAR

INPUT SHAFT

COUNTERSHAFT DRIVE GEAR

COUNTERSHAFT SECOND SPEED GEAR

Fig. 15. Transmission gears in second-speed position.

Maintenance of the driveline of your car includes making sure there is not any excessive wear in the U-joints (the area where the shaft is attached to the other components of the system). You can do this by getting under the car and shaking the shaft with both hands. There should be very little movement of the shaft when you twist it back and forth. The differential needs lubrication. Simply remove the plug located on the casing of the differential and stick your finger in the hole. If your finger comes out clean you need to add fluid.

There are two basic types of transmissions: *standard*, or manual, and *automatic*. The manual transmission has an extra foot pedal which the driver operates. This is the *clutch* and it enables the driver to select the appropriate gear for any driving situation. Automatic transmissions are more complex and initially more expensive. They shift gears automatically through the varying pressures exerted by hydraulic systems or through the use of a torque converter. The gear changes are governed by the speed of the vehicle.

At this writing a major automobile manufacturer has developed an automatic transmission overdrive. Transmission overdrive provides a gear ratio of less than 1:1. It reduces oil consumption and engine wear by requiring fewer revolutions of the engine for a given mileage than if direct drive, or high gear, is used. If, for example, you're driving at 60 mph, the engine will idle at the same speed as when you're doing 40 mph. Overdrive only works on the open highway and will have little, if any, effect on city driving.

Maintenance of the automatic transmission is an aspect that each driver should be well aware of. Transmission problems are major repairs and can be extremely expensive. Use the following steps to check out your automatic transmission:
1. Check the fluid level of the transmission by warming up the car to normal operating temperature.
2. Pull out the transmisson dipstick.
3. Note the color of the lubricant. It should be clear and red. A cloudy appearance indicates problems.
4. Smell the lubricant. If it smells like something is burning, especially like burnt cork, you definitely need to have it inspected by a professional.
5. Always be aware of any unusual noises or behavior coming from your transmission. A common problem is "slipping" of the gears. This is noticeable when the car shifts gears and you feel like there is a

hesitation on the part of the transmission to "catch up."

6. Regular maintenance includes changing the transmission fluid about every 25,000 miles due to the extreme heat and pressure to which the fluid is subjected.

There's not much maintenance related to a standard transmission. Once in a while the clutch may have to be adjusted and, if the gears feel stiff, or if they stick or slip, check the gear oil by locating the oil-level plug on the side of the transmission housing. The major problem that can develop is clutch failure. This is a matter of time and wear and is difficult to avoid or predict.

It is definitely *caveat emptor* (let the buyer beware) in the area of transmission mechanics. Before you allow any work to be done on your transmission bring your car to several shops, get a written estimate, and make sure the shop has a solid reputation. Know your guarantee. Many transmission problems can be corrected through the adjustment of the bands and linkage or the cleaning and/or replacement of the transmission filter and screen. Just because one dealer claims you need a new transmission does not mean you definitely need one. Before you decide to buy a new or rebuilt transmission make sure that you have no other alternative.

The Electrical System

alternator—The belt-driven device that produces the proper amount of electricity to operate the electrical system of the automobile and keep the battery fully charged.

ampere—The unit of measure of electricity flowing through a circuit.

arcing—The jumping of electrical current between two conductors.

charging system—The components of the engine that are responsible for keeping the battery fully charged, such as the alternator and voltage regulator.

chassis—The basic frame of the automobile.

electrical system—The system that electrically cranks the engine for starting, furnishes high-voltage sparks to the engine cylinders to ignite the fuel/air mixture, lights the lights, operates heater motor, radio, etc.

Consists, in part, of starter, wiring, battery, generator, voltage regulator, distributor and coil.

fuse—A glass-enclosed piece of metal attached between two electrical contacts. When too much current passes through the fuse, the metal melts, preventing damage to the electrical system.

gap—The precisely measured distance between two electrical contacts, such as the ignition points or spark plug electrodes.

generator—The component of the engine that produces electricity. Most modern automobiles have replaced the generator with the *alternator*, which is more efficient.

ground—The necessary attachment of an electrical system to permit the completion of an electrical circuit. Without a properly grounded system, the electricity in the system will follow the shortest path and damage the system.

ohm—A unit of measure of resistance within the electrical system.

resistance—The amount of difficulty that a wire or electrical component offers to the flow of electricity.

terminal—A point of connection in an electrical circuit.

volt—A unit of measure of electrical force.

voltage regulator—A device used in connection with the generator to keep the voltage constant and to prevent it from exceeding a predetermined maximum.

The electrical system in your car has many functions. It activates lights, gauges, buzzers, air-conditioners, tape players, radios, wipers and more. The system provides the power for all the electrical components in the car. The larger the car, the more power is necessary to operate the various accessories.

The electrical power is generated by the *alternator*, or (on older models) *generator*, as the engine runs. The power is then stored in the *battery* and is available when called upon. If there's a malfunction in the system's ability to recharge itself, you'll find yourself stuck.

We tend to take the system for granted until something goes wrong. Finding a short circuit in the electrical system can be maddening, considering that there are hundreds of feet of wire in the average car. A short circuit can develop when there's an improper connection or the insulation around a wire has frayed and the wire is touching bare metal. By testing each connection and inspecting each wire you should be able to find the problem and correct it. This is a very tedious and time-consuming job, though.

The electrical system has a major cable going from the battery to the *fuse box* (usually located under the dashboard). From there the wires run to each of the electrical components. The fuses act as safety valves. If too much power enters the system, the fuse burns out before any damage can take place in the accessory or device demanding the power. In any electrical failure, always check the fuses first—often the simple replacement of a fuse will correct a problem. Always carry an extra set of fuses in your car for such occasions.

If you blow a fuse more than once in a short period of time, you have a problem somewhere else. If you find yourself stuck without a fresh fuse and your ignition fuse blows, find a fuse in the box of the same size and amperage that's not being used at the moment (such as a headlight fuse during the daytime) and put it in the ignition fuse position. It may be enough to get you home or to a service station. (See page 75 for instructions on how to change fuses.)

The proper maintenance of the battery, starter, fan belt, etc., described in the various sections of this book will help keep your electrical system trouble-free.

The Steering System

---

idler arm—A component of the steering linkage that supports the system.

power steering—A type of steering system that reduces the amount of effort the driver has to exert to steer the car.

stabilizer bar—A component in the suspension system of some cars that prevents the car from leaning too much when the car is turning or cornering.

---

steering column—The shaft that connects the steering wheel to the other parts of the steering system. Modern cars have collapsible columns that telescope when an unusual amount of force is applied, as in an accident.

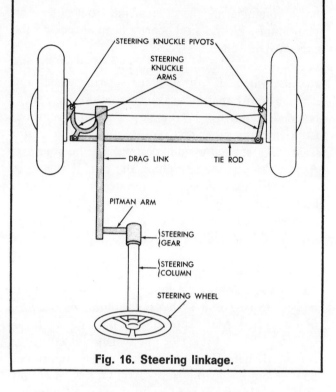

Fig. 16. Steering linkage.

Your car changes direction as you turn the steering wheel. By turning the wheel you are turning a shaft that is attached to a gearbox. Inside the gearbox the circular motion of the turning shaft is changed to a left or right directional motion.

The steering rods are attached to the gearbox. These rods are flexible and respond to the condition of the road and the action of the driver. This is accomplished through the employment of *ball joints*. Your ankle is an example of a ball joint; you can extend your foot as well as turn it from side to side. The ball joint is a mechanical copy of the same type of system and allows for the steering demands to be met as well as for the steering system to react to the road conditions.

Your major responsibility in keeping the steering system working properly is to keep the tires properly aligned (improper alignment places unnecessary pressure on one side of the steering system) and to make sure the ball joints are greased and lubricated.

If you suspect that there might be a loose ball joint or some other problem in the steering system, you can check the system by raising the front end, grasping the wheels firmly and shaking them back and forth. There should be very little play in and little noise coming from the area of the front end when you do this. Worn wheel bearings can also cause the excessive movement.

A common problem is too much "play" in the steering wheel. If you turn the steering wheel and it moves more than several inches before the system responds, tightening is necessary. Check the gearbox. Lubricate any areas that require it. There may also be a large set screw and lock nut on the gearbox. Adjust the screw and tighten the nut. If this does not end the excessive play in the steering wheel, it is best to bring your car to a professional.

Power steering systems use a "booster," or hydraulic aid, to make the steering of the car easier for the driver. You can check the mechanism by pulling out the dipstick and adding fluid if necessary. Automatic transmission fluid (ATF) is used in the power steering unit as hydraulic fluid. Also check the drive belt. Make sure the belt has only ½ to ¾ inches (12 to 19 mm) of play when pressed in the center. If there is too much play, adjust the pulley and/or power steering unit. A tell-tale sign of low fluid is a whining sound from the unit as the steering wheel is being turned.

The Lubrication System

oil filter—The element through which the oil flows to remove dirt and other impurities.

oil galleries—The passageways the oil goes through within the engine.

oil pan—The storage compartment for the engine oil. It is located underneath the engine.

oil pressure—The pressure under which the oil flows through the engine, measured in pounds per square inch.

oil pump—The component that forces the oil through the engine when the engine is operating.

viscosity—The measure of thickness and ability to flow of lubricating oil.

Friction in your engine is one of its greatest enemies. As metal rubs against metal, there's a definite tendency for the metal to increase in temperature. When metal increases in temperature, it expands. Since there's no room in an engine for this expansion, you can see that preventing this friction from developing is one of your goals in maintenance.

The lubricating system actually has four vital functions: to prevent metal-to-metal contact of the moving parts; to assist in carrying heat away from the engine; to clean the engine parts as they lubricate (unless you are driving an older car which takes only non-detergent oil); and to form a seal between the piston rings and the cylinder walls to prevent a leakage of the combustion gases and inefficient combustion.

After the oil picks up heat from its contact with pistons and cylinder walls, it drops into the *oil pan* which is underneath the engine. The flow of air past the oil pan helps to cool the oil. An *oil pump*, located near the oil pan, forces the oil through the entire system to every moving part of the engine.

The oil in your engine is its lifeblood; keeping it clean and having the proper type of oil in your engine is extremely important in keeping things going smoothly.

There are many different brands and types of oils on the market. Detergent oils clean as they lubricate, preventing a buildup of rust, corrosion or acid in the engine. A non-detergent oil simply doesn't offer this cleaning capability. When choosing an oil for your car, select known brands and read the label to make sure the oil is recommended for the type of driving you do. *MS* and *MSE* designations ensure you of the maximum protection.

Oil is also classified by *weight* or *viscosity*. The modern car owner doesn't have to be too concerned over the weight of oil in his car. Modern oils offer *multi-viscosity*, meaning that the weight of the oil changes according to temperature conditions. An oil labeled *10W-30* or *20W-40* will provide year-round protection unless you live in areas of extreme temperatures. Read the labels of oils and check your owner's manual to confirm the weight and type of oil you should use in your car and for your region.

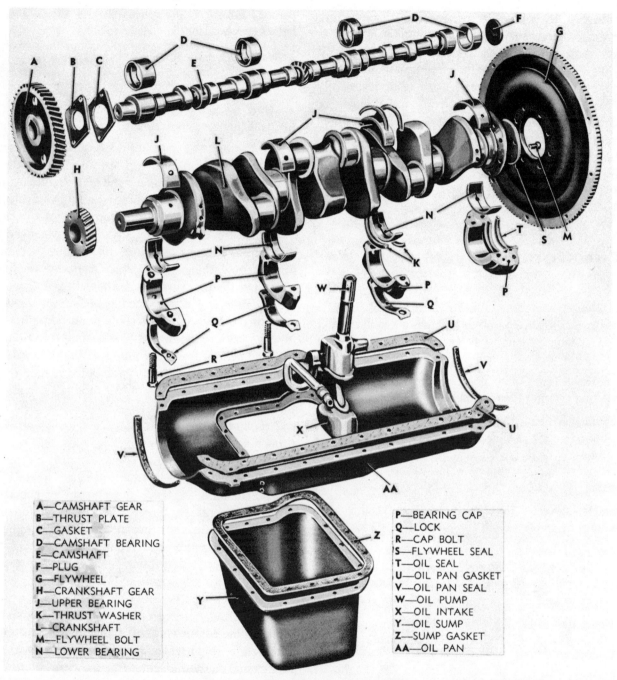

A—CAMSHAFT GEAR
B—THRUST PLATE
C—GASKET
D—CAMSHAFT BEARING
E—CAMSHAFT
F—PLUG
G—FLYWHEEL
H—CRANKSHAFT GEAR
J—UPPER BEARING
K—THRUST WASHER
L—CRANKSHAFT
M—FLYWHEEL BOLT
N—LOWER BEARING

P—BEARING CAP
Q—LOCK
R—CAP BOLT
S—FLYWHEEL SEAL
T—OIL SEAL
U—OIL PAN GASKET
V—OIL PAN SEAL
W—OIL PUMP
X—OIL INTAKE
Y—OIL SUMP
Z—SUMP GASKET
AA—OIL PAN

Fig. 17. Oil pan and lower engine parts.

Recently, synthetic and "increased-mileage" oils have been introduced to the market. These oils claim to provide better protection, reduce friction, allow for better mileage and last longer between oil changes. You may wish to try these oils, but be careful. If you find your car is burning this new oil or your performance is not up to par, switch back to your regular oil before any damage develops.

The oil in your engine is kept clean by the *oil filter*. This filter is part of the oil flow and, as the oil passes through it, traps any larger particles that may cause damage to your engine. Keeping the filter clean is as important as keeping the oil clean. Change your oil at the recommended intervals found in your owner's manual. You can change it more often, especially if you do a great deal of driving under dusty or harsh conditions. *Always change your filter when you change your oil.* You're really not saving anything by allowing the quart of dirty oil in the filter to remain in your engine.

The Cooling System

antifreeze—Ethylene glycol, a substance added to the cooling system to help prevent freezing and boiling over.

coolant—The liquid that circulates through the cooling system to keep the engine from overheating.

cooling system—The system of the engine that is responsible for keeping the engine from overheating. It consists of the radiator, water pump, thermostat, radiator cap, fan, hoses, water jackets, and drive belts.

ethylene glycol—The chemical compound commonly known as antifreeze.

fan—Multi-bladed piece of metal located behind the radiator. The fan turns by way of a pulley driven by the fan belt. Its major function is to help cool the engine when the motor is running at slow speeds.

heater hose—The flexible tube responsible for carrying coolant from the radiator to the core of the heater.

overflow—The plastic or rubber tubing that allows excess coolant to run out of the radiator without bursting the system.

radiator—The component in a water-cooled engine in which the water/coolant mixture filters through a series of small passageways to allow for the dissipation of heat.

thermostat—The temperature-sensitive component in the cooling system that opens to allow coolant to pass through the engine when necessary.

water jacket—The passages in the engine block through which the coolant circulates.

water pump—The component that pushes the coolant through the engine.

An engine that produces too much heat will eventually seize up and stop operating. It's the job of the cooling system to keep the temperature of the engine at an acceptable level to prevent overheating. It does this in the following manner.

A mixture of *ethylene glycol* and water flows through the cooling system. As the mixture (coolant) flows through the engine, it absorbs most of the heat generated there. The mixture then trickles through the *radiator* and is subjected to a flow of air that absorbs the heat and thus cools the mixture before it goes back into the engine. The coolant is circulated with the help of the *water pump*. If the water pump were to break down, the coolant would remain trapped in the different areas of the cooling system and the engine would overheat.

An engine that runs too cold also won't provide proper performance. It's the job of the *thermostat* to block the circulation of coolant until it reaches a certain temperature—normally 180°F. to 195°F. (82°C. to 91°C.). Once the coolant reaches the proper temperature, the thermostat opens and the coolant flows through the engine which continues to run at the established temperature. Should the thermostat freeze in the open position, the car would not reach proper operating temperature in cold weather. If it were to freeze shut, the engine would overheat.

When the engine is idling, the rush of air through the radiator is provided by the *fan*. The fan turns as a result of the movement of the *crankshaft* and the *fan belt* which connects them. If the fan belt is too loose or is broken, the fan will not turn fast enough and the engine will overheat.

The coolant is carried through the engine via the *water jacket*. Outside of the engine itself, the coolant is carried through the *radiator hoses*. These hoses are made of high-grade materials and are capable of withstanding tremendous heat and pressure. Once a small hole or leak develops, they lose pressure and your car overheats. Hoses should be checked regu-

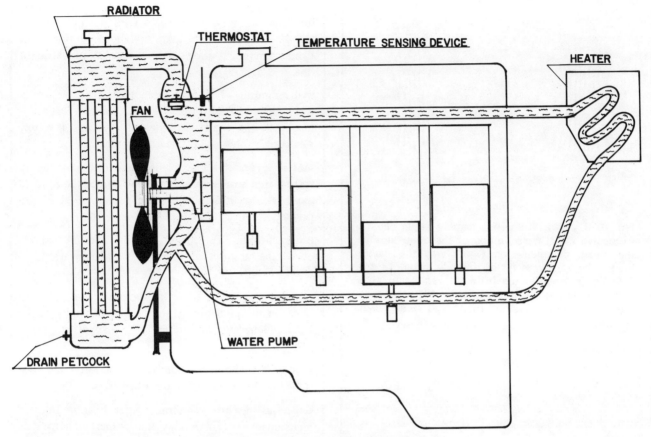

RADIATOR

THERMOSTAT

TEMPERATURE SENSING DEVICE

HEATER

FAN

WATER PUMP

DRAIN PETCOCK

Fig. 18. Components of the cooling system.

larly. They should feel firm and somewhat flexible, not weak or brittle.

The cooling system is an extremely important part of your car. An engine that runs for any length of time without the system working properly will surely cease to operate and you'll find yourself confronted with a major repair.

The Braking System

alignment—The adjustment of the front suspension and steering system so that the automobile is most stable on the road.

axle—The member of the automobile support system to which the wheels are attached.

bead—The inner area of the tire that keeps the tire attached to the wheel.

bleeding the brakes—The process of forcing air out of the brake lines.

brake drum—The metal cylinder attached to the wheel against which the brake shoes rub to stop the wheel.

brake fade—The loss of stopping power usually caused by overheating in the brake pads or linings.

brake fluid—Special liquid used in the hydraulic braking system.

brake lining—The heat-resistant material on the surfaces of the brake shoes that rubs against the brake drum to slow the motion of the wheel.

brake lockup—An overreaction of the brakes that results in skidding and loss of control of the car.

brake shoes—The moving parts of a brake system that are forced against the brake drums to slow the wheel.

camber—The vertical wheel alignment angle that involves an outward or inward tilting of the tires.

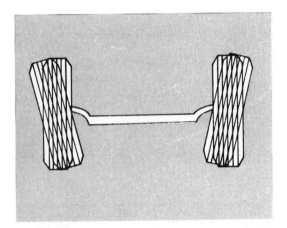

Fig. 19. Camber. The wrong camber angle causes excessive EVEN wear on one or the other side of the tread, depending on which way the wheel leans. The backward tilt of the axle structure can also cause trouble: too little tilt results in poor handling and spotty wear; unequal tilt can cause one tire to pull, resulting in uneven tread wear.

Figs. 20-21. Alignment is the angle of the wheel in relation to direction of travel. Too much toe-in (above) produces a feathered edge on the INSIDE of the tread design; too much toe-out (below) produces a feathered edge on the OUTSIDE of the tread design.

caster—The vertical wheel alignment angle that involves the forward or backward position of the tire in relation to the axle's pivot point in front. Proper alignment allows the tire to track in a straight line.

hydroplaning—The phenomenon that occurs on a wet road when the tires of the automobile lose contact with the road and ride on a layer of water, resulting in the loss of steering control.

master cylinder—The component of the braking system that stores brake fluid and forces the fluid to the brake cylinders when the brake pedal is depressed.

power brakes—A type of braking system that reduces the amount of pressure the driver needs to exert.

radials—A type of tire construction where the cord fibers in the plies are arranged at right angles to the beads. Generally considered to be a superior type of tire construction.

rear axle—The cross-member of the driveline system that the rear wheels are attached to.

self-adjusting brakes—Brakes that have a built-in mechanism that maintains the proper distance between the brake shoe (or pad) and the brake drum (or disc).

toe-in—The measurement used to describe the degree that the front wheels point at each other.

toe-out—The measurement used to describe the degree that the front wheels point away from each other.

wheel bearing—The ring at the end of the axle that accepts the weight of the car and allows the axle to turn with a minimum of friction.

wheel cylinder—The unit in the braking system that activates the brake shoes on the individual wheel. It is activated as a result of the pressure exerted through the brake fluid from the master cylinder.

Now that we have the car in motion, we may find it necessary to stop it somehow. Automobile brakes use friction to stop the forward or backward motion of the car. There are two brakes available to drivers —the *hydraulic brakes*, which stop the car under normal circumstances, and the *emergency* or *parking brake*, which is used in an emergency situation or as an assist in securing the car upon parking.

The hydraulic system works by applying pressure to a fluid that then transfers the force to the brakes. The fluid used in a braking system is a high-grade petroleum product capable of withstanding tremendous heat and pressure. Always use the highest grade of brake fluid available. Any breakdown in this area will result in brake failure.

Brake fluid is stored in a reservoir called the *master cylinder*. Cars built in the U.S. after 1967 have two cylinders—the primary cylinder, which operates under normal conditions, and a smaller secondary cylinder which acts when the primary cylinder fails. When the secondary system must be used, braking effectiveness is reduced by one half. Half a brake, however, is better than none at all.

Two brake lines come out of the master cylinder: one travels to the rear wheels and the other goes to the front wheels. They transfer the brake fluid and are linked to the wheels by the wheel cylinders. When you step on the brake you force the brake fluid into each wheel cylinder. Inside each cylinder are two pistons—one on each end—which are moved in opposite directions by the hydraulic pressure and which, at the same time, push the *brake shoes* against the *brake drum*.

Actually, there are two types of braking systems: *drum brakes* and *disc brakes*. The above describes a drum system. The brake drum is made of metal and is part of the wheel itself, revolving with it. The brake shoes are covered with a special material called *brake lining*. When you apply the brakes you are forcing the shoes against the inside of the drums and the resulting friction stops your car.

Disc brakes use pads which close on a spinning disc attached to the wheel much like your hand would clutch a record that is rolling away from you. The pads are on a hydraulic device that straddles the disc and is called a *caliper*. When you hit the brakes, the pads close on both sides of the spinning disc like your fingers close on that rolling record.

Power brakes use the vacuum created by the engine to allow more pressure to be exerted on the disc or drum. Power brakes can be sensitive at times. You should always get the "feel" of your brakes when starting out, especially when driving

a strange car. Jamming on brakes that are overly sensitive can send you and your passengers hurtling forward, possibly causing injury.

The parking or emergency brake is a mechanical device used when the hydraulic system fails, or to secure the car when parked. The brake is nothing more than a cable attached to the rear brakes and the driver engages it by pushing a pedal or pulling a lever. Much more force is necessary to stop the car using only the emergency brake. It would be wise to practice stopping your car on a deserted road to get the feel of using the emergency brake. Knowing what to expect in a time of emergency might save your life.

With a standard transmission, the idea is to plan ahead, downshift and release the gas pedal to coast to a stop. This not only saves you gas but also allows your brakes to last much longer. A quality set of brakes and proper installation can be expensive—proper care and maintenance will save you money and time.

Due to the life-and-death aspect of a properly functioning brake system, it is *not* recommended that amateurs attempt to perform any intricate work on their brakes. Any time you feel a difference in the way the braking system reacts, have it checked out by a qualified mechanic. I always insist on the highest quality in brakes and tires for my cars. My life and the lives of my family and passengers depend on them.

At this point, let's discuss tires with the braking system, to emphasize the fact that braking capability is greatly affected by the quality of the tires on your car and their condition.

The major consideration in dealing with tires is the amount of tread wear. The accepted minimum amount of tread you should have on your tires is 1/16″ (1.6 mm). An easy way to measure this is to take a Lincoln-head penny and insert it, head first, into the tread of the tire. If you can see any part of Lincoln's hair, you have inadequate tread and you should replace the tire as soon as possible.

Bald tires make for very poor road-hugging and stopping performance in the tires. A major problem is *hydroplaning*. If your tires are bald and you hit some water, the tire will skim over the water, losing contact with the road surface, causing you to lose control of the car. Tires with good tread will *slice* through the water and direct it through the grooves of the tread.

Some tire manufacturers are building tread-wear indicators in their tires. These become noticeable when the tire runs low on tread. You'll see small bars on the tire that interrupt the normal tread design. Heed these warning signs and replace the tires before you hydroplane into an accident.

A tire is made up of layers of material—usually rayon, polyester, or a like fabric—called *plies*, cords inside the rubber itself to make the tire stronger, longer lasting, and more flexible.

There are basically three types of tires available to the consumer—the *bias* ply, the *belted bias* ply, and the *radial* ply tire. The bias ply tire has some of the layers (the cords) constructed at an angle to each other so that each reinforces the other. The belted bias ply tire adds another layer or two of material (the belts), such as fiberglass or steel,

under the tread and around the circumference of the tire. This layer adds more strength to the tire.

The radial ply tire is constructed differently. It's considered the best buy in tires because of its superior road-handling ability and longevity. The radial tire is constructed with the ply (cords) of the tire going from bead to bead. This type of construction allows for less friction to develop within the tire and for lower rolling resistance. As a result, the radial tire can actually add to your gas efficiency.

The major enemy of tires is heat. In order to prevent excessive heat building up in your tires, keep them inflated properly. An under-inflated tire will "drag" and cause the tire to overheat. It will also reduce your gas mileage considerably. The under-inflated tire will wear unevenly along the edges. The over-inflated tire will be more vulnerable to road hazards as well as to excessive wear through the center of the tread.

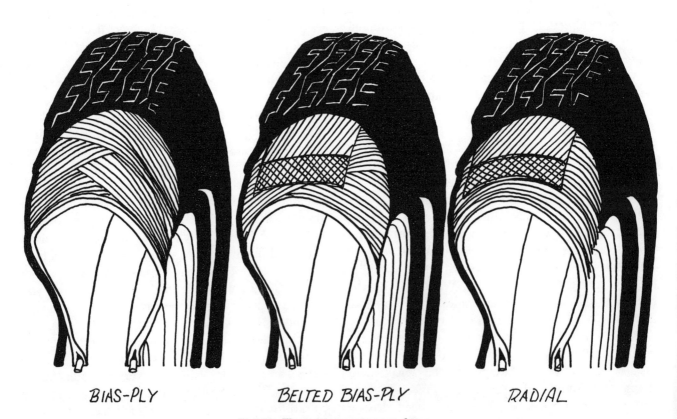

BIAS-PLY   BELTED BIAS-PLY   RADIAL

Fig. 22. Tire types—cutaway views.

Checking your *tire pressure* is an easy task. Purchase a *tire gauge* of good quality. (It has been noted that tire gauges at service stations are often inaccurate.) Check the pressure when the tires are cold; warm tires will give a false reading since the air in the tires has expanded. Be aware of changes in atmospheric temperature—for every 10°F (ca. 5°C) drop in temperature, your tires will lose one pound (70 grams) of air pressure. Follow the recommended p.s.i.—pounds per square inch (kilograms, or grams, per square centimeter)—pressure for your car and load.

Another factor in tire care is *tire balance*. If the tires are not balanced on the rim, they wear unevenly and affect performance. An unbalanced tire will make its presence felt by sending a slight vibration through the car when moving. Keeping the tires balanced is recommended for driving comfort and for better performance and safety. Have the tires balanced at a service station, since specialized equipment is necessary to insure proper balance.

Tire rotation is a controversial subject. If you feel it's to your advantage to rotate your tires, take note of the chart and procedure on pages 78 and 79.

The performance and wear of your front tires also depend on proper *alignment*. Your steering and suspension systems should be adjusted in such a way that the front tires roll in a perfectly straight line. Any misalignment will cause undue stress on the various parts of the tire and you'll lose performance and longevity.

Conclusion

This chapter is by no means all-inclusive in explaining the workings of your car. It's designed to give you a basic introduction, and any further study you care to do is up to you. By understanding the basics you'll be able to follow the rest of the material found in this book.

There are many excellent courses offered in adult schools, community colleges and private schools. Take advantage of these, since "hands-on" experience will be excellent training for when you tackle your own repair jobs.

MISCELLANEOUS TERMS

air shock—A type of shock absorber that can be adjusted to load weight by injecting air, much like a tire is inflated.

armature—A rotating part of a motor such as a starter.

automatic choke—A part of the carburetor that produces a richer mixture of fuel when the engine is cold, thus helping to provide easier starting.

bearings—The shaft support components that permit the shaft to rotate without interference and with minimum friction.

belt—The bands driven by the engine that, by way of pulleys, operate the alternator and other components of the engine. The term also refers to the material that covers the plies of a tire (such as glass-belted tires).

block—The main part of the engine that houses the cylinders and other major moving parts of the engine.

butterfly valve—A metal plate in the carburetor that resembles the wings of a butterfly. It pivots to allow air to enter the carburetor.

cam—The off-center curved area on a shaft that moves another component (such as a valve lifter) as it rotates.

camshaft—The revolving shaft that the cams are attached to.

cylinder—The area of the engine where the pistons and valves are housed.

dwell angle—The number of degrees that the distributor cam rotates while the ignition points move from fully open to fully closed.

dwell meter—The instrument used to measure the dwell angle.

engine speed—The turning rate of the crankshaft, usually measured in revolutions per minute (rpm).

exhaust manifold—The structure that connects the exhaust ports of the engine to the rest of the exhaust system.

exhaust pipe—The pipe that connects the exhaust manifold to the muffler.

exhaust port—The opening in the cylinder (controlled by the *exhaust valves*) through which exhaust gases escape to the exhaust system.

exhaust system—The parts of the engine that permit the safe removal of gases and reduce noise.

exhaust valve—The valve in each cylinder that opens to remove the gases produced by detonation.

feeler gauge—A tool comprised of pieces of metal made to precise thicknesses used in setting gaps.

firewall—The partition between the engine compartment and the passenger area.

flexible hangers—The supports that hold the exhaust system in place.

gasket—A sealing material placed between two metal surfaces and designed to prevent the leakage of fluids or gases. An example would be the head gasket located between the block and the head of the engine.

gear—A wheel with cut protrusions ("teeth") that turns other gears when the teeth are engaged.

grease fitting—The rounded components on some members of the front suspension that are designed to accept grease through a small hole.

heat range—The term that indicates the ability of a spark plug to dissipate heat. May also denote the low and high temperatures that components operate within.

horsepower—The unit of measurement that denotes the power of an engine. One horsepower is the unit of energy required to lift 550 pounds a distance of one foot in one second.

hydraulic system—A system that uses fluid under pressure to move components of the system—the prime examples being the brake system on automobiles or the service station lift that raises the automobile to allow work under the car.

hydrometer—An instrument used to measure the specific gravity of a liquid. A *battery hydrometer* tests battery fluids and thus the state of charge in the battery. An *anti-freeze hydrometer* tests the effectiveness of anti-freeze.

idiot light—The term used to denote a warning light on the instrument panel. In most instances, gauges give the driver a better understanding of the conditions within the engine.

intake valve—The valve that opens to allow air and gas into the combustion chamber.

jack—The tool used to raise the automobile off the ground to change a tire or for other minor repairs.

jack stand—Rigid metal supports that an auto should be placed on if any person is to work under the car. Much safer than the use of the jack only.

jumper cables—Two wires attached to a "live" battery and a "dead" battery in order to temporarily provide power to the dead battery. (Same as *booster cables*.)

leaf spring—Several lengths of flat steel placed on top of each other and connected to the frame and axle. Used in the rear suspension of many cars.

linkage—A series of springs, levers and rods used to connect two mechanisms such as the steering system or throttle linkage.

main bearings—The bearings that support the crankshaft.

motor mounts—The brackets that hold the engine in place within the automobile.

muffler—The component of the exhaust system that reduces the noise of the exhaust by forcing it through a series of baffles that absorb the force of the exhaust gases.

odometer—The device that tells us how far we have traveled. Part of the speedometer.

PCV (positive crankcase ventilation) valve—Part of the automobile's emission control system, it directs unburned vapors from the crankcase into the cylinders where they are burned up in combustion.

resonator—A secondary muffler found on larger cars to help control the noise and emissions.

seal—A flexible material placed between metal surfaces to prevent the leakage of liquids.

shock absorber—The part of the suspension system that absorbs the impact of bumps and road hazards to help smooth the ride of the auto.

suspension system—The various components that support the car on the axles or wheels.

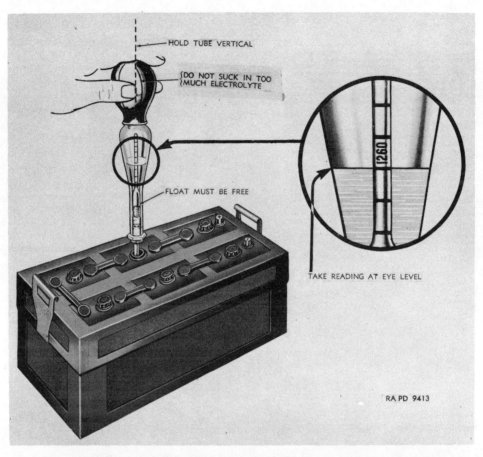

HOLD TUBE VERTICAL

DO NOT SUCK IN TOO
MUCH ELECTROLYTE

FLOAT MUST BE FREE

1260

TAKE READING AT EYE LEVEL

RA PD 9413

Fig. 23. Taking specific gravity reading of a battery with a hydrometer.

tachometer—An instrument used to measure the revolutions per minute of a running engine.

tailpipe—The last section of piping in the exhaust system.

U-bolt—A clamp, shaped like the letter "U", that is generally used in holding parts of the exhaust system in place.

universal joint—A flexible coupling that allows two rotating shafts to be attached to each other.

vacuum advance—A unit on the distributor that enables the timing to change as the engine speed changes.

Chapter Two

EMERGENCY REPAIRS
AND TROUBLESHOOTING

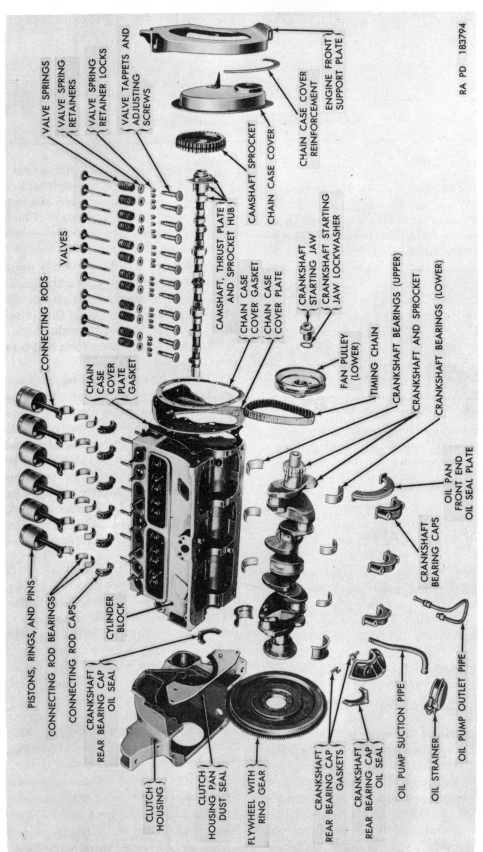

Fig. 24. Cylinder block and components of a 6-cylinder, L-head, liquid-cooled engine.

RA PD 183794

Emergency Troubleshooting

There is a basic emergency tool and parts kit that you should keep in your car. The following is a list of materials that should be included in your emergency kit:

- Jumper cables
- Flares
- Flashlight
- Duct tape
- Tire inflator (can)
- Paper clip
- Screwdrivers (flathead and Phillips)
- Electrical tape
- Adjustable pliers
- Wire
- Siphon pump
- Fan belt (make sure it's the proper size for your car)
- Plastic bag (for carrying water)
- Spark plug wrench
- Can of high-quality brake fluid
- Several clean pieces of cloth
- Small change (to phone for help when necessary)

The troubleshooting charts that follow are designed to provide you with an easy reference to some of the problems that you may encounter. If you perform the indicated checks and tests and still can't find the problem, seek professional help. Following the charts you'll find some step-by-step procedures for minor emergency repairs. In most cases, these are only temporary and should be used only until you're able to fix the car properly or have it repaired professionally.

Canvas

IGNITION TROUBLESHOOTING

PROBLEM	CAUSE	CHECK	SOLUTION
Car dead (no response from turning the key)	Battery connections	Turn on lights. If lights are dim, check battery cables at terminals.	Remove any corrosion and tighten connections.
	Loose fan belt—battery dead, as a result	See if belt is loose. Check lights. If lights are dim and terminal connections clean, your battery's dead.	Adjust belt to proper tension (page 61). Jump starting should get you going again.
	Starter connection	Battery cable leading to starter.	Clean and/or tighten all connections.
	Defective solenoid	Jump terminals across starter. Place a screwdriver across the two bolts at the top of the solenoid (see page 60).	If car starts, replace solenoid as soon as possible.
	Jammed starter	If you hear a clicking sound, the starter may be jammed.	Push car forward 2 or 3 feet (1 m) while in high gear (manual transmission) or drive (automatic). Try starting again.

IGNITION TROUBLESHOOTING (cont.)

PROBLEM	CAUSE	CHECK	SOLUTION
(Car dead, cont.)	Ignition switch	Make sure car is in "park" and/or seat belt sensors are not disconnected.	Jiggle gearshift lever and/or connect seat belts.
		Connections behind ignition key.	Push in connectors and loose wires directly behind key.
	Ignition fuse	Fuse box.	Replace fuse with one of the same size and amperage (page 75). If necessary, use a fuse of the same size from an accessory not in use at the time, such as headlight fuse during daylight.
Noise from starter but car does not start	Dampness in system causing short circuit	Look for water or condensation on wires, coil, distributor.	Remove distributor cap and wipe dry with clean, absorbent cloth.

IGNITION TROUBLESHOOTING (cont.)

PROBLEM	CAUSE	CHECK	SOLUTION
(Noise from starter, cont.)	Fouled or defective spark plugs	Pull out ignition wire leading to one of the spark plugs. Insulate yourself with one of the rags and place an elongated paper clip in the boot of the wire. Hold the wire near bare metal and have someone turn the key. If a spark jumps across to the bare metal—over ³⁄₈" (9.6 cm) —one or more of the spark plugs are at fault.	Pull out spark plugs and clean. You can use the striking surface of a matchbook cover to scrape the plugs. A road map folded in four thicknesses will provide you with a workable gap. It's also possible to close the gap on one or two plugs to about half normal. This will make the car run rough, though.
	Defective points	Remove distributor cap and check points for pitting (burning on surface areas).	Lightly scrape between points with empty matchbook striking surface.
	Defective condenser	Remove condenser but leave wire attached. With *all* electrical components *off* but the ignition *on*, touch the condenser to the housing on the distributor. If there is a spark, the condenser is defective.	Replace condenser with one of proper size (pages 89-90).

———— IGNITION TROUBLESHOOTING (cont.) ————

PROBLEM	CAUSE	CHECK	SOLUTION
Engine "seized"; will not run	Overheating	Check oil and coolant levels.	Allow to cool before trying to start. *Do not* put cold water in an over-heated radiator.

Fig. 25. The coolant level should always be approximately 1″ (25.4 mm) below the filler neck. Always remember to be careful when removing the radiator cap. Never remove it when the engine is hot.

FUEL SYSTEM TROUBLESHOOTING

PROBLEM	CAUSE	CHECK	SOLUTION
Plenty of power from ignition system but car still does not start	Lack of fuel	Do you have gas in the tank?	Add gas.
	Leak in fuel line	Visually check gas line for any leaks. Check for odor of gasoline.	Tighten any connections or unkink dents in fuel line (page 62).
	Clogged fuel line and/or fuel filter	Remove air filter and place hand over top of carburetor. Crank engine. Your hand should get wet with fuel. If it doesn't, the fuel is not reaching the carburetor.	Remove fuel filter and replace with a new one (page 83). In an emergency, you can reattach fuel lines without a filter, but a new filter should be installed as soon as possible. If lines are still clogged, have them blown out with compressed air at a service station.
	Stuck float valve in carburetor	Same test as above.	Tap side of carburetor with handle of screwdriver. This should dislodge stuck valve.

FUEL SYSTEM TROUBLESHOOTING (cont.)

PROBLEM	CAUSE	CHECK	SOLUTION
(Car does not start, cont.)	Clogged vent in gas tank	Same as above.	Remove gas cap to allow air into tank. If vent is clogged, replace cap. You can use clogged cap in an emergency by placing it loosely on the tank.
	Faulty fuel pump	Same as above.	Replace with new or rebuilt pump.
Carburetor sputters during acceleration	Engine not warmed up	Thermostat.	Replace if faulty (pages 74-75).
	Fuel being delivered in spurts	Accelerator pump.	Replace if faulty (refer to mechanic).
Engine idles too fast	Too much fuel being delivered	Choke may be stuck or idle cam set too high.	Unstick with screwdriver, clean with spray cleaner. Or reset idle cam.

—— FUEL SYSTEM TROUBLESHOOTING (cont.) ——

PROBLEM	CAUSE	CHECK	SOLUTION
Engine warm but frequently stalls	Not enough fuel being delivered	Idle speed.	Reset (refer to mechanic).
Acceleration slow—hesitation	Obstruction in throttle linkage (mechanical springs and levers)	Visually inspect system.	Remove any materials blocking movement.
	Timing misadjusted	Reset timing (pages 90-91).	Have timing checked with proper instruments.
Poor mileage (see also Chapter Five)	Leak in fuel system	Visually check all connections and gas tank for leaks.	Tighten connections or plug leaks.
	Idle speed set too high	Idle speed.	Reset (pages 83-84).

FUEL SYSTEM TROUBLESHOOTING (cont.)

PROBLEM	CAUSE	CHECK	SOLUTION
(Poor mileage, cont.)	Car is overloaded	Excess weight.	Remove excess weight and/or distribute weight more evenly throughout car.
	Air-conditioner in constant use	Do you need it on?	Limit usage.
	You may need a tune-up	All parts of the ignition and fuel system.	Tune it up (pages 68-69).
	Low tire pressure	Check all tires.	Inflate to proper pressure.
	Front end out of alignment	Alignment.	Correct (refer to mechanic).

FUEL SYSTEM TROUBLESHOOTING (cont.)

PROBLEM	CAUSE	CHECK	SOLUTION
(Poor mileage, cont.)	Clogged fuel filter and/or air filter	Remove filters and check for dirt.	Replace (pages 82 and 83).
Car continues to run after ignition is turned off (dieseling)	Low octane gas	See owner's manual for proper octane needed.	Purchase tankful of higher octane fuel.
	Spark plugs fouled	Remove and check for fouling and for proper gap (pages 86-87).	Replace as necessary (page 86).
Frequent stalling when coming to a stop	Float valve or choke stuck	Test as above (page 38).	See above (page 38).
	Idle speed too low	Idle speed.	Reset (refer to mechanic).

FUEL SYSTEM TROUBLESHOOTING (cont.)

PROBLEM	CAUSE	CHECK	SOLUTION
(Frequent stalling, cont.)	Moisture in gas tank or fuel line	White smoke from exhaust.	Add any brand of dry gas to fuel.
	Foreign substance in fuel	Fuel filter.	Replace filter (page 83).
	Air vent in gas cap clogged	See above (page 39).	See above (page 39).
Loss of power	Fuel pump not working to capacity	Fuel pump.	Replace or have rebuilt.
	Fuel filter clogged	Fuel filter.	Replace (page 83).
	Need a tune-up	Points and spark plugs.	Tune it up (pages 68-69).

NOISE TROUBLESHOOTING

Note: Pay attention to the noises made by your car. Whenever there's a change in the performance of your car or you hear a strange or different noise, your car is trying to tell you something. Heed the warning and catch the problem early, before major repairs are required.

PROBLEM	CAUSE	CHECK	SOLUTION
Rattling sound during acceleration	Bad gasoline or low octane	See above (page 42).	See above (page 42).
	Timing mis-set	Timing.	Reset (pages 90-91).
High-pitched squeal when revving the engine	Loose fan belt	Test belt (page 61).	Adjust (page 61).
Squeal when steering wheel is turned sharply	Low level in steering fluid reservoir	Pull out dipstick and check level (page 92).	Fill to proper level.
	Air in power steering system	Noise continues after filling with fluid to capacity.	Bleed system (refer to mechanic.

NOISE TROUBLESHOOTING (cont.)

PROBLEM	CAUSE	CHECK	SOLUTION
Grinding noise from corner of car—loudness depends on speed	Worn wheel bearing	Check professionally.	Have tightened, lubricated, or replaced as necessary.
Grinding noise when brakes are applied	Worn brake linings	Check professionally.	Adjust or replace as necessary.
Loud thumping at one or more corners of the car	Loose or broken shock absorbers or motor mounts	Check visually.	Repair and/or replace as necessary (pages 80-81).
Loud exhaust	Hole in muffler or exhaust system	Check visually.	Repair and/or replace as necessary.
Loud exhaust noise from under hood	Cracked exhaust manifold	Check visually.	Replace professionally.

— NOISE TROUBLESHOOTING (cont.) —

PROBLEM	CAUSE	CHECK	SOLUTION
Thumping noise when steering wheel is turned	Loose steering linkage	Check professionally.	Repair and/or replace.
Thumping noise when going over bumps	Worn ball joints	Check professionally.	Replace if defective.
Squealing noise from tires when moving at low speeds	Air pressure in tires too low	Check pressure with tire gauge.	Inflate to proper pressure.
	Wheels out of alignment	Check professionally.	Adjust alignment.
Steady knocking when revving engine	Worn pistons or bearings	Check professionally.	Possible to use heavier weight oil. Do not accelerate too fast. Extreme change in noise level indicates a major problem.

NOISE TROUBLESHOOTING (cont.)

PROBLEM	CAUSE	CHECK	SOLUTION
Constant ticking noise, depending on speed	Oil not reaching valves	Check oil level (page 82).	Add oil to proper level.
	Valves out of adjustment	Check professionally.	Repair or replace.
Turn signal blinks fast or not at all	Fuse or bulb burned out	Check visually.	Replace (pages 75-76).
	Flasher unit burned out	Most likely cause if bulbs and fuse are o.k.	Replace (page 77).
Horn does not sound	Bad connections	Check visually.	Clean all connections.
	Fuse burned out	Check visually.	Replace (page 75).

NOISE TROUBLESHOOTING (cont.)

PROBLEM	CAUSE	CHECK	SOLUTION
Squeaking when car bounces	Suspension joints need lubrication	Check professionally.	Lubricate.
Backfiring	Leak in exhaust system	Check visually.	Repair leak.
	Timing too fast/slow	Timing.	Adjust (page 90-91).

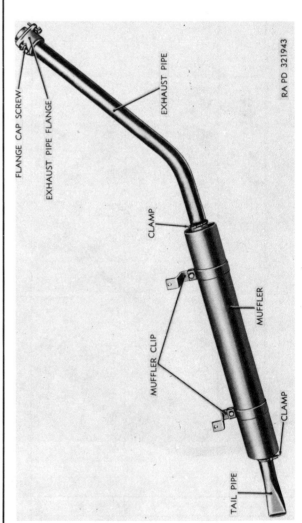

Fig. 26. **Muffler and exhaust pipe.**

FLANGE CAP SCREW

EXHAUST PIPE FLANGE

EXHAUST PIPE

RA PD 321943

CLAMP

MUFFLER

MUFFLER CLIP

CLAMP

TAIL PIPE

BRAKE SYSTEM TROUBLESHOOTING

PROBLEM	CAUSE	CHECK	SOLUTION
Pedal travels farther than normal—more than 3 inches (7.5 cm)	Low fluid level	Master cylinder (page 77).	Refill (pages 77-78).
	Brakes worn	Check professionally.	Adjust or replace.
	Air in haudraulic system	Check professionally.	Have system bled.
Pedal goes to floor	No fluid	Master cylinder.	Fill with fluid or rebuild master cylinder if necessary.
Much more pressure needed for braking than usual	Glazed linings	Check professionally.	Grind or replace.
	Power-brake pump malfunction	Check professionally.	Repair or replace.

BRAKE SYSTEM TROUBLESHOOTING (cont.)

PROBLEM	CAUSE	CHECK	SOLUTION
Emergency brake malfunction	Loose cable	Pull up brake and try to drive forward—brake should hold.	Have cable professionally adjusted.
Car pulls to one side while braking	One side of brake adjusted too tightly	Check professionally.	Adjust.
	Tire pressure uneven	Check pressure.	Inflate to proper pressure.
	Wheels out of alignment	Check professionally.	Adjust (refer to mechanic).

COOLING SYSTEM TROUBLESHOOTING

PROBLEM	CAUSE	CHECK	SOLUTION
Loss of coolant	Leak	Check system visually.	Plug leak or replace worn hoses (pages 58-59, 74).
Overheating	Loose fan belt	Test belt (page 61).	Adjust.
	Loss of pressure in system	Radiator cap.	Replace.
	Clogged radiator	Open radiator cap and observe if water is moving when car reaches normal operating temperature.	Clean and flush (pages 72-73).
	Heater clogged	Turn on and check for proper function.	Have heater blown out with compressed air.
	Hoses collapsing	Feel hoses by hand—if too soft, this may be the problem.	Replace (page 74).

COOLING SYSTEM TROUBLESHOOTING (cont.)

PROBLEM	CAUSE	CHECK	SOLUTION
Heater broken	Clogged	Not functioning.	Have heater blown out with compressed air.
	Blower not operating	Electrical connections.	Tighten and/or clean.
		Blockage in fan area.	Clear blockage.

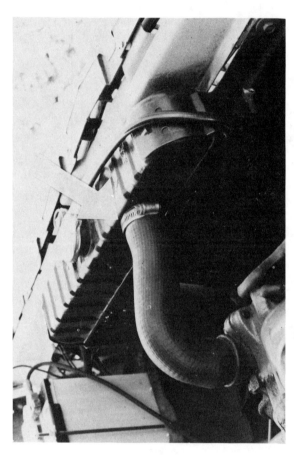

Fig. 27. Replacing a radiator hose is a simple task: just remove the clamps (arrow) at each end, replace the hose with a new one, and replace the clamps.

Dashboard Troubleshooting

The major components of your automobile engine are constantly being monitored by the lights and/or gauges that can be found on your instrument panel.

Gauges are more accurate than lights. If you have the option of ordering either for your car, you may find that gauges let you keep a closer watch on the conditions in your engine. In order for a warning light to operate, the malfunction must already have occurred. For example, let's see what happens if your car's running low on oil (something that no car owner should ever allow to happen). The engine will be low on oil *before* the warning light comes on. If the driver had an oil pressure gauge, it would warn him when the oil *begins* to run low—not after it's already hit the low level. That's why warning lights are referred to as "idiot lights."

The following chart will help you to understand the lights and/or gauges that are on your car. As a test, all your warning lights should glow when the ignition key is turned to the "start" position and go out when you release the key. This is a safeguard against the presence of a defective bulb. Always check these lights when you start your car. If a light doesn't glow when the key is turned, have the bulb checked.

DASHBOARD TROUBLESHOOTING

PROBLEM	CAUSE	CHECK	SOLUTION
Oil warning light stays on (or oil gauge reads "low")	Shortage of oil	Check oil (page 82).	Add oil.
	Broken oil pump	Take off the valve cover and start engine (this can be very messy—*do not* perform this test in your driveway or garage). Oil should rise to valve area.	Replace pump if necessary.
	Blocked oil lines	Remove valve cover and check oil lines for blockage or thick sludge.	Flush the oil lines with a commercial solvent made for this purpose. Ask the attendant at your auto parts store for the proper solvent.
Oil warning light goes out when engine speed is increased (or gauge indicates higher pressure when engine speed is increased)	Shortage of oil	Check oil.	Add oil.
	Not enough oil pressure at low speeds	Condition may persist if oil level is o.k.	Professional help needed.

DASHBOARD TROUBLESHOOTING (cont.)

PROBLEM	CAUSE	CHECK	SOLUTION
Alternator light remains on (or ammeter reads "discharge") even when engine is running above idle speed	Fan belt broken or loose	Visually check fan belt. Test adjustment (page 61).	Replace or adjust (page 61).
	Loose or broken wire from alternator	Check for loose or broken wires visually.	Reconnect wires. Be careful— ■ Stop engine ■ Connecting wrong wires will damage parts.
	Voltage regulator broken	Needs professional testing equipment.	Replace.
	Alternator broken	Needs professional testing equipment.	Replace.

DASHBOARD TROUBLESHOOTING (cont.)

PROBLEM	CAUSE	CHECK	SOLUTION
Fuel gauge reads "low" too frequently or too suddenly	Leak in fuel tank or along fuel lines	Visual inspection.	Plug leak or tighten fuel line connections.
	Someone siphoned gas out of your car	None of the above are at fault.	Purchase locking gas cap or other anti-siphoning device.
	NEVER CARRY EXTRA FUEL IN TRUNK OR PASSENGER COMPARTMENT!!!		
Brake warning light remains lit or goes on while car is moving (practice stopping your car under this condition—AVOID PANIC)	Leak in brake lines	Visual inspection.	Repair lines.
	Shortage of brake fluid	Check level in master cylinder.	Replace fluid (pages 77-78).
	Leak in master cylinder	Visual inspection.	Replace or rebuild master cylinder.

DASHBOARD TROUBLESHOOTING (cont.)

PROBLEM	CAUSE	CHECK	SOLUTION
Temperature gauge reads "high" (or light glows)	Lack of coolant	Check level in radiator (*CAUTION:* Make sure engine is cool before you attempt to remove radiator cap.)	Replace coolant.
	Leak in cooling system	Visual inspection.	Tighten (or replace) connections or hoses.
	Car is overloaded or towing too much weight	All of the above are not at fault.	Lighten load.

Emergency Repairs

The following directions are here to help you in case your car breaks down. Use them as necessary. You'll also find methods to get you going again in the preceding troubleshooting charts.

JUMP STARTING

A large number of road service calls result in no more than the motorist receiving a jump start from the driver of a tow truck. This can be expensive. By buying your own jumper cables, you'll recover their cost the first time you use them.

A car will need to be jump-started under any of the following conditions:

- The alternator belt is loose, resulting in a run-down battery.
- Corrosion has prevented the battery from being recharged.
- The battery is old and run-down.

The following is the proper procedure for jump-starting your car. Be careful and follow the steps in the order given.

1. Do not allow the donor car and the dead car to touch. Make sure both cars are in "park" or neutral, parking brakes are set, lights and other electrical accessories are off and the ignitions are off.

2. Make sure both batteries are of the same size (voltage).

3. Make sure that one terminal of each battery is grounded. Normally this is the negative (—) terminal. This means that a wire runs from the negative terminal directly to the engine block or to the frame of the car.

4. Add water to any of the battery cells on both batteries that are low.

5. If a battery has frozen fluid inside, *do not* attempt to jump it. Gases may be trapped in the ice and can cause an explosion.

6. Attach the red jumper cable to the dead battery's positive (+) terminal. Then attach the end of the cable to the positive terminal of the donor battery.

7. Attach the black jumper cable to the negative terminal of the donor battery and attach the other end to a bare metal part of the dead car's engine block. This completes the circuit and may spark. *It is imperative that this last connection be as far away from the battery as possible to prevent the spark from igniting any gases in or near the battery. Keep all cables away from any fans or moving parts. Do not touch black cables to red cables.*

8. Attempt to start the dead car. If it doesn't start, start the donor car and allow it to run for a few minutes. Try to start the dead car with the donor car running.

9. Once the dead car starts, remove the cables in exactly the opposite order from which they were placed on the batteries. The cable farthest away from the battery might spark; it should be removed first.

Be careful! A battery can explode. If you follow all the directions in order, you should be on your way in a few minutes. If you can't start the car in this manner, refer to the troubleshooting chart for other possible causes.

MENDING A LEAKY HOSE

The first thing to do if your car overheats is to check the cooling system for leaks. *Wait for the engine to cool before opening the radiator cap.* The coolant in the system is under tremendous pressure and can spray steam onto your face and upper body. You can relieve the pressure by pushing the safety release valve on your reclamation system, if you have one. If your car doesn't have one, you can easily install one yourself. Some radiator caps are equipped with a safety valve. Just lift the valve *carefully* if you have this type of cap. If a garden hose is available, you can spray cold water into the front of the radiator to help cool the coolant faster.

If you're simply low on water, *do not* pour water into the hot engine—this can crack the seams of the radiator. Pour water into the radiator only after the engine has cooled. Pour it in *with the engine running* to spread the cooler water evenly throughout the system, thus preventing cracked seams.

If your fan belt is broken, wait for the engine to cool. You can drive *slowly* with a broken fan belt,

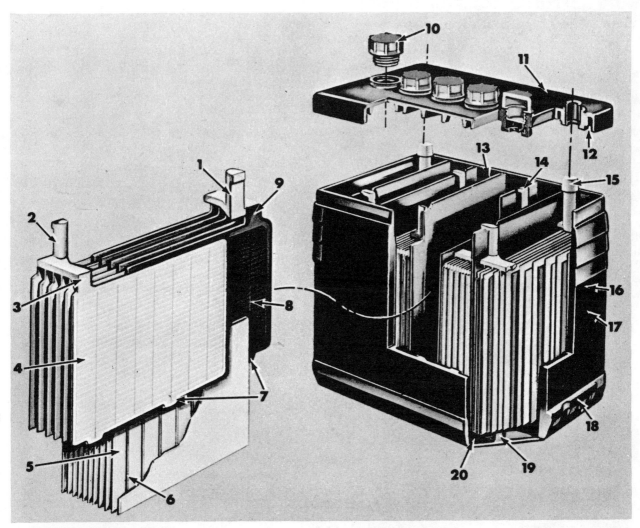

Fig. 28. Battery components:

1. Positive cell terminal and strap
2. Negative cell terminal and strap
3. Negative terminal lug
4. Negative plate (grid and sponge lead)
5. Separator
6. Separator rib
7. Plate feet
8. Positive plate (grid and lead dioxide)
9. Positive terminal lug
10. Vent plug
11. One-piece cover
12. Epoxy resin sealing lip
13. Cell partition
14. Over-partition connector
15. Terminal post
16. Container
17. Ampere-hour rating
18. Mounting ledge
19. Element rest
20. Sediment space

but only for short distances. Your battery may be discharged, however.

Should you find a leak in a hose, follow the directions below to get you going. This is a temporary repair and you should have the hose replaced as soon as possible.

1. Allow the engine to cool.

2. Clean all dust, dirt and grease from the area of the hose.

3. Using the duct tape from your emergency kit, tape the area of the leak, making sure you overlap the tape to insure strength.

4. Keep the radiator cap loosened one notch and drive *slowly* until you have the hose fixed. Loosening the cap will relieve the pressure from the hose.

BY-PASSING THE SOLENOID

The solenoid is an electrical switch that acts as a temporary booster increasing the power from the battery to activate the starter motor when you turn the key. If your car doesn't start properly and it seems like the starter is not getting enough of a "kick" to start the engine, the problem could very well be the solenoid.

To check the operation of the solenoid:

1. Locate the solenoid (normally attached to the top of the starter motor). Also note if there are any starter relay switches between the battery and the solenoid.

2. Check all the connections to the starter relays and the solenoid itself. Make sure they are tight, dry, and clean.

3. Using a well-insulated screwdriver, thereby insulating yourself as well, place the metal section of the screwdriver across the terminals of the solenoid, making sure that contact is made.

4. Have another person turn on the ignition. If the car starts easily you probably need to replace the solenoid. If the car still acts the same, then the solenoid is not at fault and you should check all the other parts of the ignition system. Knowing that the solenoid is at fault is much cheaper than having the mechanic talk you into purchasing a new starter or entire electrical system.

Beware: When bridging the solenoid be very careful not to have your hands, hair, or clothing in an area where they could be caught up in the engine.

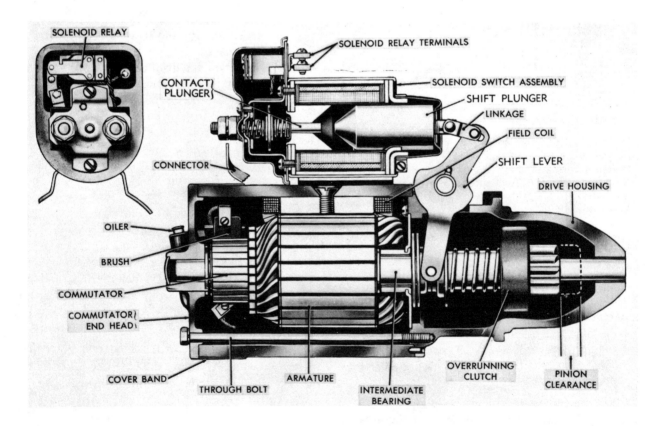

Fig. 29. Solenoid shift starter with overrunning clutch.

FAN BELT REPLACEMENT

If you find yourself with a broken fan belt, you'll be able to drive a short distance on the power stored in the battery. Any other broken belt (air conditioning, power steering) won't disable your car—you'll just loose the function of these accessories. If you don't replace it immediately, be sure you remove it so that it doesn't tangle the other belts and pulleys.

If you find that you don't have a fan belt of proper size in your emergency kit, it's possible to use a lady's stocking or panty hose to act as a temporary fan belt until you can replace it with a proper belt. (If any man reading this decides it might be wise to store a pair of hose in his glove compartment, I highly recommend that you inform your wife or girlfriend first. Failure to do so may result in serious injury unrelated to your car.)

It's a simple matter to replace a fan belt on a car that doesn't have a number of different belts to drive various accessories. If your fan belt is on the inside of a number of belts, it will be necessary to remove the belts in front of the fan belt before you can get going

again. Here's the procedure for replacing a fan and alternator belt. Any other belt can be replaced in a similar manner.

1. Remove the old belt, making sure you know how it ran around the different pulleys.
2. Loosen the easiest adjustment bolt to reach and slide the alternator toward the engine.
3. Put the new belt in position. If necessary, pry it onto the tracks of the pulley using a screwdriver.
4. Adjust the belt by sliding the alternator outward along the adjustment track.
5. Holding the belt tight, retighten the adjustment bolt and check the tension. You should have less than ½″ (12.7 mm) of play in the center of the longest stretch of belt between pulleys.

The best way to avoid being forced to replace a fan belt in an emergency situation is to keep a periodic visual check on the condition of the fan belt and replace it as soon as there are any signs of fraying or breaking. Inevitably, the belt will break on some rainy night when you're dressed up for an evening on the town.

Fig. 30. To adjust a loose fan belt, loosen bolt on the slide track (arrow) and retighten it after moving the alternator outward on the track.

INSULATING SHORTED WIRES

One type of breakdown that can be very easy to fix is an ignition or coil wire short-circuit. If this happens, you can use the electrical tape in your emergency tool kit. *Make sure the ignition is off*, then clean the wire area by wiping with a clean cloth. *Do not* separate any wires within the frayed insulation. After cleaning, wrap the tape around the area of the fray, making sure you overlap the tape.

If you don't have tape available, you can use a handkerchief or piece of string to "sling" the frayed wire. Simply position the wire in such a way that it doesn't touch any bare metal parts. Then tie the string or handkerchief in such a way that it cradles the wire to prevent it from touching the bare metal. This should get you going until you can replace the wire with a new one.

UNKINKING A FUEL LINE

It doesn't happen often, but it's possible for a rock or foreign object to bounce up under your car and flatten your fuel line. This will prevent the gas from going from the fuel tank to the carburetor in sufficient quantities.

If you inspect the fuel line and find this to be the problem, it's a simple task to round off the line with a pair of pliers. Just press gently across the dent. *Be careful not to break the line.* Have the line checked by a qualified mechanic to determine if you've sufficiently corrected the damage. Many carburetor troubles can be traced to this type of problem.

CURING VAPOR LOCK

On a hot summer day, you may find that after you've filled your empty gas tank and done some shopping, your car suddenly refuses to start. Of course you bought some ice cream and if you don't get it home quickly it'll become ice mush. What can be the problem?

When gasoline comes out of the ground, it's cold. Very cold, in fact. It's like water coming out of a deep well. If your engine is at normal operating temperature and your tank was almost empty, it's possible that the new gas will be called upon to run the engine before it's had a chance to warm up. This cold gas will get into the hot fuel line or fuel pump and condensation will occur as the drastic change in temperature causes the fuel to boil.

The best approach is to open the hood of the car and allow the engine to cool down and release the vapor bubbles in the line. If this takes too long (don't forget the ice cream is melting) it's possible to dunk a piece of cloth in some water and drape it over the fuel pump. The reduction in temperature will speed the cooling-down process. If you still can't get going, relax and eat the ice cream before it's ruined.

THE ULTIMATE BREAKDOWN — THE STOLEN CAR

There's nothing worse than coming out of a restaurant or a movie theater to find that your prized chariot is missing. If you are afraid that your car may be stolen, there are many different devices that you can buy to protect your car, ranging from sirens to bells to electrical shocks for those who touch your car.

The most economical method to use, though, is also the simplest. Just take the rotor out of your distributor cap (see Fig. 61, page 88) after parking the car. This will break your ignition circuit and the car won't be able to start without another rotor. Keep the rotor in your pocket until you return. The trick now is *not* to have your rotor stolen . . . or your car towed away.

BATTERY TIPS

■ Along with keeping the water level properly maintained, keeping the battery clean and dry is essential for maximizing battery life. Check the terminals periodically for corrosion build-up. Corrosion frequently shorts-out a full charged battery —corroded terminals is the first problem to check for if the starter fails to work and the headlights won't come on.

■ If you have to add water regularly to one or two cells, the battery may have a cracked case. But if all or most of the cells require water more than every 1000 miles or so, the battery is probably overcharging. Have the voltage regulator checked out to prevent severe battery damage.

■ Check the generator/alternator belt regularly for proper tension. A loose or glazed belt can run down a battery quickly.

■ Keep the engine properly tuned to reduce the starting load on the battery.

■ Get in the habit of turning off all accessories every time you start the car.

■ When starting a cold car, place the transmission in neutral and disengage the clutch to reduce the starting drag.

■ Avoid slow speed and short-distance driving that doesn't give the battery time to charge back up after a start—especially in winter when the battery has to work harder to start the engine.

■ Try and limit the use of accessories when driving in stop-and-go traffic.

■ If you don't plan to use your car for a week or so in cold weather, remove the battery and store it in a warm place to prevent it from discharging and possibly freezing. Wrap the battery in old rags to prevent acid damage to the area in which it's stored.

Fig. 31. Having a cracked battery or open battery cells is not only dangerous, but your battery can become discharged if any foreign matter dilutes the acid.

Chapter Three

SIMPLE REPAIRS AND MAINTENANCE

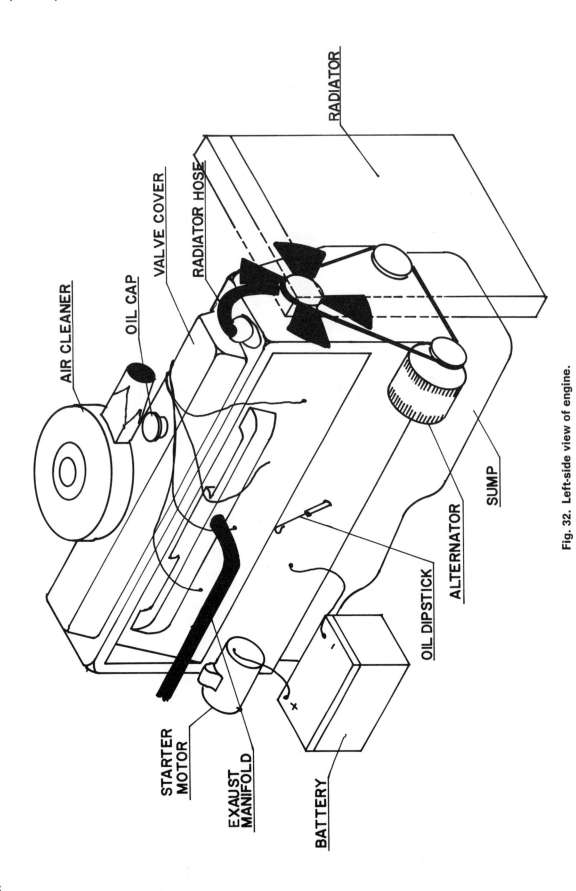

Fig. 32. Left-side view of engine.

Read the list of minor auto repairs below. Add up the amount of money you've spent over the past year to have a mechanic perform these functions on your car. If you're the average automobile owner, you've wasted over half of the money you spent.

- Oil change
- Check/replace radiator hoses and thermostat
- Change air filter
- Change fuel filter
- Replace/clean spark plugs
- Replace/clean points, condenser and rotor
- Battery maintenance
- Tire change and rotation
- Flush cooling system/replace anti-freeze
- Replace ignition wires
- Check/replace brake fluid

If you perform the above procedures on your car, you'll find that it doesn't take a tremendous knowledge of mechanical matters. You'll not only save money by doing the work yourself, but you'll learn much more about the performance of your car, and your ability to notice potential major problems will be enhanced. You'll be able to spot problems and correct them before they become critical.

Auto parts are expensive if you purchase them through a dealer or mechanic. He has to impose a service charge to order the parts and pick them up at the parts store. Sometimes the cost of these parts is double what you really have to pay for them if you know where and how to shop (see Chapter 4). Keep your eye on newspapers and advertising flyers that promote sales in your local discount stores and chain auto supply houses.

Planning ahead can save you money, too. As you get into the habit of doing the maintenance work

on your car, there will be certain items that you'll need from time to time, such as oil, filters, spark plugs, etc. By buying these items when they're on sale, even if you don't plan to do the work immediately, you'll save money over the regular price and avoid the inevitable price increases. For example, some people, especially if they have more than one car, like to buy oil by the case whenever it's on sale. The case of oil may last them a year or more, but the savings are usually significant, especially these days.

When you purchase supplies for your car, it's always best to get brands that are well known and guaranteed. If something is wrong, you can always return them for replacement or refund. When ordering parts, make sure that they're made to fit the make, model and year of your car. If you're not sure the parts will fit, don't be afraid to ask the salespeople for help.

Tools

If you're serious about working on your own car, it is necessary to maintain a basic tool kit. The following is a list of the tools you'll need to perform the basic repairs mentioned in this chapter:

Screwdrivers (Phillips and flathead)
Set of wrenches (open-end and box)
Socket set
Oil filter wrench
Feeler gauge
Spark plug gap gauge (round-wire type)
Spark plug wrench
Wire brush
Pliers
Spark plug file
Battery hydrometer
Coolant hydrometer
Tool box

Fig. 33. A basic set of tools is all that's required for most backyard work.

As time progresses you may decide to try more complex repairs for which you'll need more complex and expensive tools. The above list is minimal and will permit you to perform basic repairs.

A word of caution: *Read your owner's manual* before attempting any repairs. Your manual contains valuable information on the location of various parts of your car and the refill capacity of the various systems that you'll be concerned with. Furthermore, whenever you're not sure of what you're doing, don't hesitate to seek help. Don't cause more damage because of pride.

Tune-Ups

Unfortunately there is no industry-wide standard that defines exactly what a tune-up is. What one mechanic may consider a tune-up may not be considered a tune-up by another. For this reason, the

steps listed below should be considered as a tune-up by definition. Should you bring your car to a shop or decide to do it yourself, this is what should be done:

1. Spark plugs removed. Cleaned and gapped or replaced (pages 86-87).
2. Ignition cables inspected for wear, fraying, or cracks. Replaced if necessary (pages 84-86).
3. Installation of new points and replacement of the condenser (pages 89-90). (For cars with electronic ignition the above is not necessary.)
4. Inspection of the distributor cap for cracks. Replacement if necessary.
5. Battery terminals cleaned (pages 71-72). Battery tested with a voltmeter.
6. Compression test on all cylinders (pages 96-97).
7. Ignition timing checked. Timing adjusted if necessary (pages 90-91).
8. Fuel pump tested for proper operation. Fuel filter cleaned or replaced (page 83).
9. Air filter cleaned or replaced (page 82).
10. Carburetor, choke and linkage checked and

cleaned. Fuel mixture adjusted for maximum economy (pages 83-84).

11. Fan belt and other drive belts checked for proper tension and/or wear. Replaced if necessary (page 61).

12. Radiator hoses checked for wear or leakage. Replaced if necessary (page 74).

13. Emission controls checked and adjusted.

14. PCV valve checked and replaced (pages 92-93).

15. Oil change and oil filter replacement (pages 81-82).

16. Coolant checked.

17. Brakes, master cylinder, and brake lines checked.

18. Chassis lubricated.

19. Exhaust system checked and tested for leaks.

20. Windshield wipers checked and washer fluid replaced.

21. Accessories checked for proper operation.

22. Alignment checked. Tires checked for proper air pressure and for wear and tear.

The purpose of the tune-up is to keep the car in top condition, to prevent major problems, for better efficiency, to provide a more comfortable ride and for the safety of the driver and the passengers.

There are a number of rip-offs associated with the auto tune-up industry. You can protect yourself by following the explanations found in another part of this book (Chapter 4). Most importantly, do not permit any repairs that you believe to be unnecessary, ask for all replaced parts to be returned to you, and remember that knowledge is your best friend.

Safety

When you decide to work on your automobile, there's one factor that must constantly be kept in mind—the safety factor. Too many accidents occur when someone forgets or ignores a basic rule of safety. For this reason, the following points are presented to remind you that working on your car can be dangerous.

Knowing the jacking capability of your equipment is very important. Make sure that the tool you use to raise your car is able to withstand the pressure and weight of the car. If you must go under the car, *never* do so with the car supported by only a bumper or scissors jack. These jacks are designed for minor emergency situations and are to be used under those circumstances *only*. Any slight jostle may send the car crashing down on you.

Jack stands are inexpensive supports that will hold the weight of the car safely, or you may be able to find suitable materials in your yard to hold the weight of the car for you. A number of solid cinder blocks will do the trick. Make sure the car is level and balanced solidly before you crawl under it. The ideal situation for the "Saturday mechanic" is the use of car ramps. These ramps are designed to hold the weight of the car and allow you to work under it with plenty of room to move about.

No smoking! When working near an automobile you must always keep in mind that you are near flammable and explosive materials that can ignite and cause serious injury. Make sure that you keep lighted cigarettes, cigars, pipes and any other smoking material away from the work area. One mistake could be the mistake of your life. The same goes for the use of tools that can spark or cause a high degree of friction. For example, if you attempt to patch a hole in your muffler by using an electric drill or sander to clean the area of the hole, be absolutely certain that there are no leaks or gasoline fumes near the gas tank.

Be aware of the properties of gasoline. It can explode and cause serious damage to a person or to property within the area of the explosion. The best way to stop a gasoline fire is to smother it. *DO NOT* spray water directly on the fire since the gasoline will float on the water and you'll do nothing more than spread the fire.

Gasoline vapor is also flammable. If you don't store gasoline in a proper air-tight container, the fumes may leak into the air and travel a fair distance to be lighted by a heat source or spark. *Never* store gasoline in the house or the garage of your home. This practice is like keeping several sticks of dynamite in your home. *Never* carry extra gasoline in the trunk of your car. Rear-end collisions are common and the gasoline can be thrown all over the area and ignite.

After gasoline has burned in an engine, it can still be dangerous. The main component of an automobile's exhaust is carbon monoxide. This gas is odorless, colorless and tasteless. It is also deadly. When you work on your car, *always* work in a well

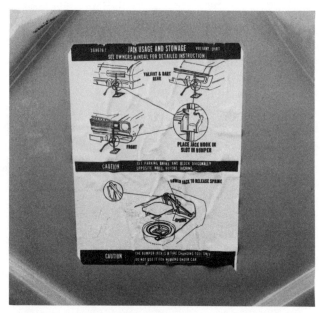

Fig. 34. Jacking instructions for your car will most likely be found on the underside of the trunk lid.

ventilated area. *Never* work in your garage, even with the door wide open, if the engine has to be run for any length of time. Car ports may also trap carbon monoxide and cause damage to yourself and others. *Never* leave a hole in the passenger compartment of your car through which exhaust fumes can leak into the car. Driving with carbon monoxide entering your car is like driving your own personal gas chamber.

When you're working on your car, always have proper lighting in the area. If you can't see what you're doing, you can not only damage your car, but you may also hurt yourself in the process. Make sure you can see everything clearly. You may wish to buy an inexpensive mechanic's light that plugs into a regular wall outlet and has a protective wire mesh over the bulb as well as a hook from which to hang the light.

If you're doing a job that involves any amount of danger, it would be a good idea to have a friend standing by who can help you if the need arises. Should an accident occur, your friend will be able to help you or obtain help if necessary.

Keeping the area clean is another safety factor that must be kept in mind. A serious injury can result from tripping over a wrench left on the floor or by starting the engine when a tool has been left in

the area of the fan. Keep all your tools clean and in their proper place. Also remember to lock your tool box or put it where small children will not be able to get into it. Make sure that any grease or oil spilled on the floor or driveway is wiped up immediately and completely. Sawdust or sand will soak up oil or grease and it's a simple task to sweep or shovel the mixture into a proper container.

When working on your car, try to wear clothes that are somewhat tight-fitting. A baggy sleeve or trouser leg can easily get caught up in an engine and cause serious injury. The same goes for long hair. If you have long hair, it will be to your advantage to wear a hat with the hair tucked underneath, or to keep your hair tied behind your head or in a bun. Long hair can not only get caught in the workings of an engine, but it may also block your vision if it gets in your eyes. Hair is also flammable, especially "afro" hair styles.

Mention also has to be made of eye protection. A pair of plastic goggles is an inexpensive insurance policy when it comes to the protection of your eyesight. Batteries, for example, are filled with acid. Any contact with skin or eyes can be very dangerous.

The preceding was not intended to scare you; only to make you aware of the possible dangers that may exist. Please keep these concepts in mind and be careful. Safety is a family affair.

REVIEW OF SAFETY FACTORS

- Know the jacking capability of your equipment.
- Make sure car is steady and balanced if you must go under it.
- Do not smoke.
- Respect the volatile nature of gasoline at all times.
- Remember the danger of carbon monoxide.
- Maintain proper lighting.
- Use the buddy system for dangerous repairs.
- Keep the work area clean to avoid mishaps.
- Do not wear baggy clothes.
- Keep hair out of the way.
- Protect your eyes and skin.

Battery Maintenance

PURPOSE

To insure a reliable burst of power when starting the automobile.

MATERIALS

Screwdriver
Wrench
Sandpaper
Cloth
Lightweight grease

(WARNING: AUTOMOBILE BATTERIES CONTAIN ACID. AVOID ALL CONTACT WITH EYES, SKIN AND CLOTHING.)

PROCEDURE

1. Locate battery, alternator, and alternator belt (it's usually the same one that drives the fan).
2. Check the condition of the battery cables—make sure there's no corrosion on the cable clamps or battery posts and that the cables are attached tightly and fully to the posts.
3. To remove corrosion:
   a. Remove the clamps and lightly sandpaper clamps and posts. If there's a large amount of corrosion buildup, use the end of a screwdriver to scrape clean. There are also stiff wire brushes available at modest cost and that are specifically designed to clean battery posts and clamps.
   b. If there's an excessive buildup of corrosion, mix approximately 4 tablespoons of baking soda in an 8-ounce (240 ml) glass of water. Pour the mixture gently onto the posts and clamps. Allow the mixture to eat away the corrosion, then flush with clean water and wipe dry.
   c. Secure clean cables to clean posts tightly. Wipe the battery dry.
      WARNING—Do not allow any water or baking soda mixture to find its way into the cells of the battery. This will neutralize the cells and discharge the battery.
   d. Smear a light coat of lightweight grease (petroleum jelly is fine) on the clamp and post to prevent corrosion buildup.
4. Check the battery water level by opening the vent holes. The water level should be up to the bottom of the fill spout. If you need fluid, use distilled water and bring each cell of the battery up to level—don't overfill. If you have one of the newer sealed batteries, this procedure is unnecessary.

Fig. 35. Clean and tight-fitting terminals ensure a quick, efficient start.

5. To adjust the fan and/or alternator belt:
   a. The "play" of the belt should be ½″ to ¾″ (12.7 to 19 mm) when you press on the middle of the belt with your finger.
   b. Another sign that the belt may be loose is a loud squealing noise when the engine is revved.
   c. To tighten a loose belt, find the slide rail of the alternator or one of the pulleys (see Fig. 30). Loosen the bolt and slide the alternator

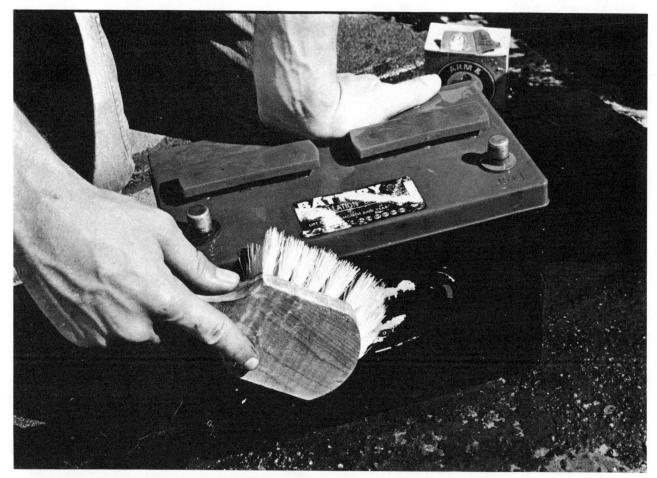

Fig. 36. Periodic removal and washing of the entire battery with a baking soda solution will prevent dirt from discharging the battery. The case should be thoroughly rinsed and dried before reinsallation.

or pulley in such a way as to tighten the belt (away from the engine). Hold the alternator or pulley steady and retighten the bolt. Check the play again.

Flush Cooling System/ Replace Anti-Freeze

PURPOSE

To insure that the engine will not freeze, breaking the block and causing extensive damage, and to provide the engine with enough cooling capacity to prevent overheating.

MATERIALS

Pliers
Pan to catch coolant
Can of radiator flush
Replacement anti-freeze (if necessary)
Access to water hose (garden hoses do just fine)

PROCEDURE

1. Park the car on a slight incline, if possible, with the front of the car facing downward. This helps drainage.
2. Place a pan under the radiator so that the coolant will drain into it when the plug is removed.
3. Loosen the drainage plug, but *do not* remove it. Loosen it enough so that you can turn it by hand.

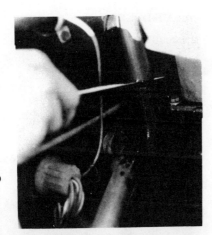

Figs. 37 and 38. Installing a kit to flush the cooling system requires only cutting a heater hose and installing a T-fitting.

12. Start the engine again and allow the water to remain at the full level by adjusting the water going into the top of the radiator. This will remove unwanted materials from the cooling system. Keep the engine running until the liquid flowing out of the drain is clear.

13. Allow all the water to drain out of the radiator.

14. Replace the drainage plug making sure you *do not* overtighten.

15. Pour anti-freeze into the empty radiator. Check your owner's manual or the label on the anti-freeze container to note the proper mixture of water and anti-freeze.

16. After adding the proper amount of anti-freeze, fill the radiator with water.

17. Run the engine for several minutes, checking to make sure the radiator remains full. Check for leaks.

18. Stop the engine and replace the radiator cap.

19. If your car has a recovery system (a small plastic container with a hose coming from the top of the radiator), remove the container and flush it out with clear water. Fill the container with water about half-way and replace it in its proper location.

There are also a number of kits on the market for flushing the cooling system that make the job quite easy. Follow the instructions provided by the kit manufacturer.

4. Remove the radiator cap. *CAUTION: Never* remove the cap when the engine is hot. Steam may spray onto your body, causing severe injury.

5. Start the engine and allow it to run until it reaches normal operating temperature (about 10 minutes).

6. Stop the engine and open the drainage plug to permit the coolant to drain out.

7. When the radiator is empty, replace the drainage plug and add the radiator flush through top of radiator.

8. Fill the rest of the radiator with water from the hose.

9. Start the engine again and let it run for about 10 minutes or for the length of time recommended on the label of radiator flush. Keep your eye on the level of water in the radiator and add water when it looks low.

10. Stop the engine. Open the drain plug again and let the mixture of flush and water drain out.

11. Close drain and fill the cooling system with water from the hose. After the system is filled, open the drain and adjust the flow of water going into the top of the radiator from the hose to match the water flowing out of the drain.

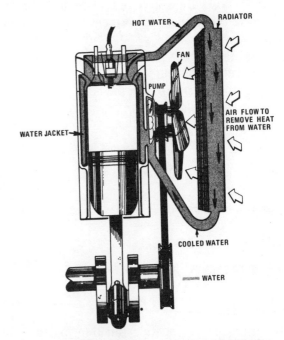

Fig. 39. Water flow between radiator and cylinder.

Check/Replace Radiator Hoses

PURPOSE

To insure proper operation of the cooling system and prevent the failure of a hose.

MATERIALS

Replacement hoses (if necessary)
Flathead or Phillips screwdriver
Pliers
Replacement hose clamps (if necessary)
Pan to catch coolant

PROCEDURE

1. Locate the radiator hoses. There are generally two—one coming from the top of the radiator and one coming from the bottom.
2. Open the radiator drain (petcock) to remove all the coolant, catching it so it can be poured back in later.
3. While the car is warm, but not hot, press the hoses with your fingers. If the hoses are brittle or very spongy, they're probably in need of replacement.
4. If the hoses are in need of replacement, make sure you have the proper replacement hoses for your car model and year.
5. Find the clamps that hold the hoses to the radiator and engine block.
6. Remove the clamps and the hose.
7. Replace coolant. Insert new hose and tighten securely. Start engine and check for leaks.

Check/Replace Thermostat

PURPOSE

To insure proper heating function and to prevent overheating.

MATERIALS

Replacement thermostat and gasket
Screwdriver(s)
Replacement hose clamps
Pan to catch coolant

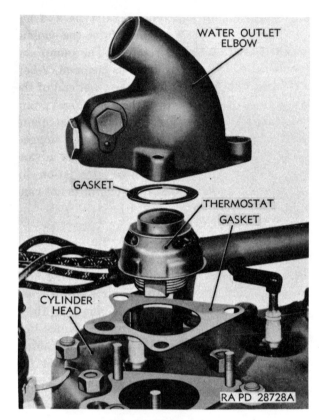

Fig. 40. Thermostat.

PROCEDURE

1. Locate the thermostat, normally at the engine end of the top radiator hose (Fig. 40).
2. Drain approximately 2 quarts of coolant from the system through the drainage petcock at the bottom of the radiator.
3. Remove the radiator hose and the thermostat.
4. Boil some water in a saucepan. Drop the thermostat in the boiling water. If it opens (the coil section expands), the thermostat is working properly.
5. If the thermostat does not open, replace it with the new part, making sure it is the right size and is

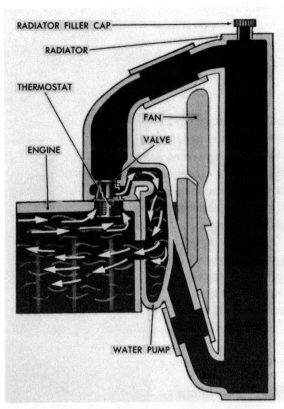

Fig. 41. When the engine is cold, a valve controlled by the thermostat prevents the water from flowing through the radiator (shown). When the water reaches a certain temperature, the valve opens and the water flows through the radiator to be cooled.

MATERIALS

Replacement fuses—always carry extras for emergency situations
Fuse puller

PROCEDURE

1. Locate fuse box.
2. Remove the fuse labeled for the type of problem you have. Pull it away from metal clips. Since fuses break fairly easily, you may wish to add a fuse puller to your tool kit. This inexpensive tool makes the job safer and easier.
3. Look inside the glass tube. If the metal strip is broken, the fuse must be replaced by another of the same size and amperage rating.
4. Put a replacement fuse in and try the electrical system that failed.
5. If fuse blows again, there's a major problem with the system that must be checked.

Be careful of the type of fuse you buy. Some fuses on the market are delayed-action or "slow-blow" fuses. Most fuses burn out as soon as they're hit by too much current, but a delayed-action fuse can withstand a brief surge of current before burning. Delayed-action fuses are not recommended for most automotive uses, since even a short surge of power can damage some electrical components. You may, however, be able to use a delayed-action fuse in an air-conditioning system where the initial pull of energy may burn out regular, fast-acting fuses, especially when the air-conditioner is in constant use. If you're not sure of what type of fuse to buy for a particular application, check your owner's manual or ask the attendant at your auto parts store.

facing the right direction. *Always* use a new gasket when changing a thermostat.
6. Slide the hose back into place and secure.
7. Replace the coolant.
8. Start up the engine and check for any leaks.

Replacing Fuses

PURPOSE

Whenever an electrical system fails, check the fuses first. Fuses can be found under the dashboard or by checking your owner's manual.

Replacing Bulbs

PURPOSE

To replace burned-out headlights, directional signals and parking lights.

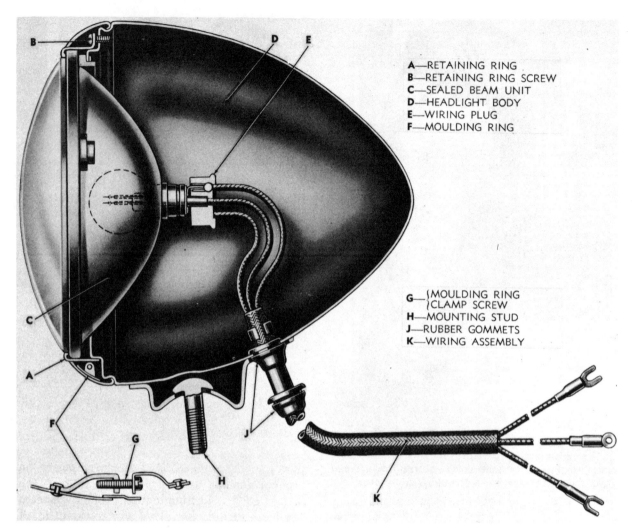

A—RETAINING RING
B—RETAINING RING SCREW
C—SEALED BEAM UNIT
D—HEADLIGHT BODY
E—WIRING PLUG
F—MOULDING RING

G— {MOULDING RING
{CLAMP SCREW
H—MOUNTING STUD
J—RUBBER GOMMETS
K—WIRING ASSEMBLY

Fig. 42. Headlight assembly.

MATERIALS

Replacement bulbs (check to make sure of correct size)

Screwdriver(s)

PROCEDURE

1. Test all the lights. (Brake lights can be checked without help by backing close to a wall or garage door and applying the brakes. The reflection will be visible in the rearview mirror.)

2. *Headlights*—Unscrew the trim area around the headlight. *Do not* touch the screws inside the trim area. These are adjustment screws and will put your lights out of alignment if tampered with. Remove the

headlight and detach the socket behind it. Most lights have three prongs set at angles to each other. Make sure the replacement bulb has exactly the same prongs. Secure the new bulb and reset into the trim area. Replace the trim and secure with the screws. Test the bulb to make sure it operates properly and has been installed correctly.

3. *Directionals and brake lights*—Remove the plastic covering by unscrewing the holding screws. Once the bulb is accessible, push the bulb into the socket and then twist counter-clockwise. The bulb should then be easily removed. Insert the new bulb by pushing it down into the socket and twisting clockwise. Replace the plastic covering and test the bulb.

Replacing Flasher

PURPOSE

Replacement of the electrical component that causes the directional signals to blink.

MATERIALS

Replacement flasher

PROCEDURE

1. Locate the flasher (normally behind instrument panel). An easy way to locate the flasher is to listen to the noise it makes when it is in proper working order. If you can't see it, move your hand around carefully touching the instruments. The flasher will be the object in which you can feel the clicking sound.
2. Once located, just pull the flasher straight out of its socket.
3. Replace by inserting the new flasher into the vacant socket.

Figs. 43 and 44. The master cylinder. Check your brake fluid level by lifting the cover. Notice the two reservoirs: the second reservoir will take over in case the first one malfunctions.

Check/Replace Brake Fluid

PURPOSE

To insure that the proper amount of hydraulic fluid is in the brake system to avoid brake failure.

MATERIALS

Flathead screwdriver
Replacement fluid (make sure you buy only high-grade, heavy-duty fluid!)

PROCEDURE

1. Locate the master cylinder (Figs. 43 and 44).
2. Try to remove the spring clip from the top of the cylinder by pushing with your fingers. If you can't remove the clip, use the screwdriver to pry the clip away from the cylinder.

3. Carefully remove the top cover making sure no foreign material falls into the reservoir.
4. Gently push the rubber gasket back into place in the top of the lid.

77

5. Fill the reservoir up to approximately ¼″ (6.3 mm) below the top of the reservoir.

6. Carefully replace the lid and snap the clip back into place.

If the car needs a great deal of fluid, there's a distinct possibility that something is seriously wrong with your brake system. Have it looked at by a qualified mechanic.

7. Replace the lug nuts carefully *by hand only.*

8. Lower the car.

9. Tighten the lug nuts with the tire iron as tight as possible.

10. Replace hub cap.

11. Have the flat tire fixed as soon as possible. It's not a good idea to drive around without a spare.

Tire Changing

PURPOSE

To replace a damaged tire.

MATERIALS

Jack
Tire iron
Wheel blocks

When changing a flat tire, keep the following safety rules in mind:

■ Ask all passengers to leave the car.
■ Make sure you're far enough off the road so that you won't present a hazard to other motorists.
■ Make sure the car is resting on a flat area.
■ Engage the parking brake.
■ Use your emergency flashers to warn oncoming motorists.
■ Block the tire diagonally opposite the tire being replaced.

PROCEDURE

1. Remove the tools and spare tire from the trunk.

2. Remove the hub cap using the sharp end of the tire iron.

3. Loosen the lug nuts while the tire is still on the ground.

4. Jack up the car following the instructions in your owner's manual.

5. Remove the lug nuts. Use the hub cap as a receptacle for them—*do not lose the lug nuts.*

6. Remove the tire and place the new tire on the wheel *carefully.*

Fig. 45. When replacing the lug nuts, follow the "star pattern" (Fig. 47) to ensure an even tightening of all the nuts.

USING THE SPARE

NOT USING THE SPARE

Fig. 46. Five-tire rotation (including the spare) at 5000-mile intervals is good economics as well as a good safety practice.

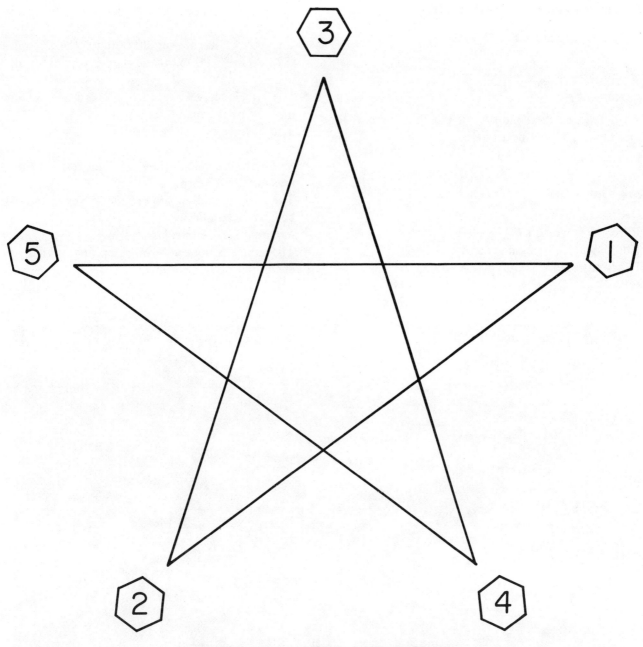

Fig. 47. The "star pattern" for tightening lug nuts.

Tire Rotation

Rotating your tires every 5,000 to 6,000 miles (8,000 to 9,600 km) will prolong the life of the tires and give you better performance. Follow the simple diagrams here (Fig. 46) and remember that there is a major difference between rotating radial tires and conventional tires. *Never* use radial and conventional tires on the same automobile. Radial tires will hold the road much better and can cause a conventional tire to pop off the bead during a high-speed turn if the latter is on the same axle.

Checking/Replacing Shock Absorbers

PURPOSE

To determine the condition of the shock absorbers and replace them if necessary.

MATERIALS

Replacement shocks
Proper size wrenches
Equipment for blocking and supporting car
Penetrating oil

Check the following and replace your shock absorbers if:

- The shocks have over 20,000 to 25,000 miles (32,000 to 37,000 km) and they're original equipment.
- The shocks have exceeded the mileage recommended by the manufacturer.
- You observe oil on the barrel of the shock absorber.
- Shake the shock absorber. If it moves, the bushings inside are worn.
- The tires are badly worn or scuffed, yet should still be in good condition.
- Your car lacks control in steering.
- The car "hits bottom" when stopping suddenly or encountering large bumps.

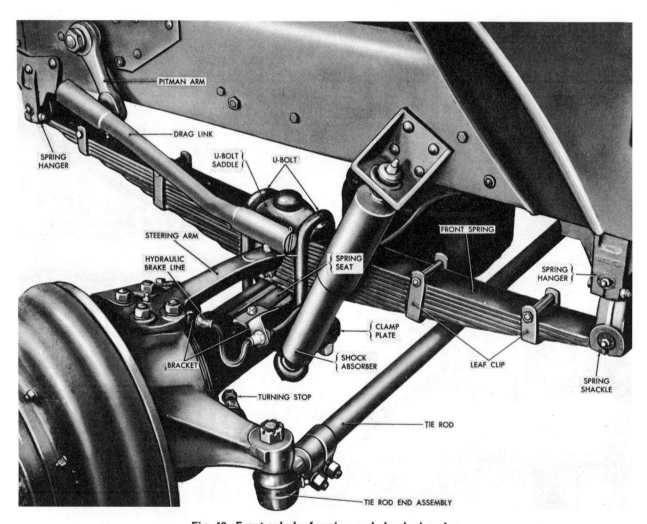

Fig. 48. Front axle leaf spring and shock absorber.

- Large dents or broken rods are visible on the shock.
- Try the push-bounce test. Push down on each corner of the car several times in succession, letting go of the car on the downward push. The car should not bounce more than 1½ times.

If the shocks are to be replaced, change both shocks on the same axle (both front or both rear). Remember that new shock absorbers will not correct the problems created by unbalanced tires, bad bearings, worn front end parts, or weak springs.

PROCEDURE

1. Read the installation instructions found on the shock absorber carton.
2. Make sure the car and front or rear axles are supported. *Do not* let the rear or front wheels "hang." Also support the springs since the tension of the shock absorber holds the springs in place.
3. If rust is apparent on the shock studs, scrape with a wire brush and apply penetrating oil at least one day in advance of performing the work.
4. Take note of the mounting hardware. Replace the hardware in the same positions when the new shock is installed.
5. Remove the upper hardware first, then pull the shock from below after removing the lower hardware.
6. Make certain that brake and fuel lines are not in the way of the operation of the new shock.
7. Install the new shocks according to manufacturer's instructions. *Do not* over-tighten. Steel-type mountings should not be tightened to the point where the rubber bushings are wider than the washers.

Changing the Oil

PURPOSE

To replace old worn-out oil that may have lost its ability to lubricate and clean properly.

MATERIALS

New filter (make sure the new filter replaces your old filter according to manufacturer's specifications)
Wrench to fit drain plug on oil pan
Oil filter wrench
Receptacle for old oil
Cloth

Fig. 49. Putting oil in your car is simple. Just remove the oil filler cap and pour the oil in.

PROCEDURE

1. Run the engine for several minutes until it reaches operating temperature, then turn it off.
2. Locate the drain plug on the oil pan.
3. Remove the plug by turning it counter-clockwise.
4. Allow the old oil to drain into the receptacle.
5. Locate the oil filter and remove it using the oil filter wrench.
6. Wipe off the area where the filter touches the engine.
7. Rub a small amount of clean oil onto the rubber gasket around the opening of the new filter. This allows the filter to seat properly.
8. Screw on the new filter *carefully*. Once it touches the engine, turn the filter by hand another half turn. *Do not* use the filter wrench when installing an oil filter.

CHECKING YOUR OIL

Since a number of problems can be caused by a low oil level, it's important that you know how to check your oil accurately. Most people don't realize that there's more to it than just pulling out the dipstick:

1. Run the engine until it reaches normal operating temperature. Checking your oil level when the engine is cold will not give you a true reading.

2. Shut off the engine. (Make sure that the car is *on level ground*!)

3. Wait a few minutes for all of the oil to flow into the oil pan.

4. Remove the dipstick, wipe it off, and re-insert it *completely*.

5. Pull out the dipstick again and read the oil level.

6. Add oil if the level is down by one quart or more. *Don't* add oil if the level is down less than a quart. You're actually better off being down half a quart than if you overfill by that amount. Too much oil will create excess pressure in the system and this will cause the oil to foam, thereby reducing lubrication.

If your car consistently loses oil, it is either burning it excessively or losing it via a leak. The symptom of burning oil is too much smoke from the exhaust system. Have this checked professionally.

The most common sites for oil leaks are the valve cover gasket (between the valve cover and cylinder head), the oil pan gasket (between the oil pan and engine block), and the oil filter gasket (between oil filter and engine). The simplest way to check for leaks is to clean the area around the suspected leak with engine cleaner, then visually check for leaking oil while the engine is running.

Caution: Be extremely careful getting under the car while the engine is running. Keep the transmission in "Park," block the wheels of the car, and have a friend sit in the car with his foot on the brake. And be aware of moving parts and belts!

---

9. Replace the drain plug carefully so as not to strip the threads.

10. Add the new oil.

11. Run the engine for approximately 10 minutes and check all areas for possible leaks.

12. Wipe all tools clean.

Air Filter Replacement

PURPOSE

To replace the old filter to allow clean air to reach the carburetor in sufficient amount.

MATERIALS

Pliers
New filter (make sure the new filter replaces your old filter according to manufacturer's specifications)

PROCEDURE

1. Locate the air filter (see Figs. 5 and 6, page 10).

2. Remove the wing nut on top of the filter housing by hand. If the wing nut is too tight, carefully use pliers.

3. Remove the top of the housing, being careful not to damage or disconnect any attached hoses (these are part of the pollution control system).

4. If you have the replaceable paper filter, remove it and either replace it with a new one or clean it by vacuuming or by blowing compressed air through it from the inside out.

5. If you have the type of filter that has a flexible cover, remove the cover and clean it in dishwashing liquid and warm water, making sure to let it dry thoroughly before proceeding. Squeeze the cover and soak it in oil. Remove excess oil by squeezing the cover firmly.

6. Replace the cover over the filter area.

7. Replace the cover of the air filter housing and hand-tighten the wing nut to secure it.

Fuel Filter Replacement

PURPOSE

Replace a clogged or dirty filter that may be restricting the flow of gas into the carburetor.

MATERIALS

Pliers or screwdriver
New filter (again make sure the new filter is the proper replacement for the make, model, and year of your car)
Cloth

PROCEDURE

1. Locate the old filter (check your owner's manual).
2. Remove the clamps on each end of the filter housing. Slide the clamps away from the filter onto the feeding hose.
3. Wipe the ends of the fuel line hose to remove any dirt. Make sure no dirt gets into the ends of the line while it's detached from the fuel filter.
4. Place the new filter in line, making sure it's oriented in the direction of flow of the fuel. This is normally indicated by an arrow on the side of the filter itself.
5. Replace the clamps and tighten them.

Fig. 50. The fuel filter (arrow) can usually be found along the fuel line.

Most cars have the type of fuel filter (in-line) pictured below, but many General Motors cars use a steel gas line and have the fuel filter located in the carburetor housing. Replace these as follows:

1. Using the proper size wrench, unscrew the nut connecting the fuel line to the carburetor inlet. Remove the fuel line.
2. Behind the nut you just removed is another, larger one; this is the inlet fitting. Remove it and take out the fuel filter and spring. Note: the inlet fitting can be tight and difficult to remove. Use the proper size box wrench to avoid rounding off the fitting.
3. Put the new filter in place, making sure that it's aligned in the same direction as the old one was. Also replace the spring, if any, in its previous position.
4. Replace the inlet fitting. Caution: *do not over-tighten.* The inlet fitting is usually made of a harder metal than the carburetor housing and over-tightening will strip the housing's threads, causing fuel to leak from the carburetor and necessitating professional repair.
5. Re-attach the fuel line and run the engine to check for leaks.

Adjusting the Carburetor

PURPOSE

To assure the proper operation and peak efficiency of the carburetor.

MATERIALS

Tachometer
Screwdriver

PROCEDURE

1. Bring the engine to normal operating temperature.
2. Connect the tachometer as directed by the manufacturer.
3. Locate the idle-mixture screw, normally found near the base of the carburetor.
4. Turn the idle-mixture screw clockwise until engine begins to falter.

5. Turn the idle-mixture screw back (counter-clockwise) one full turn. You have set the mixture.

6. Locate the throttle-linkage screw (attached to spring return).

7. Turning this screw clockwise increases the idle speed; counter-clockwise decreases idle speed.

8. Note the needle on the tachometer. Normal idle speed is 500 rpm for many eight-cylinder engines, 600 rpm for six-cylinders. Older cars will need higher idle speeds to run smoothly.

PRECAUTIONS

- Cars with automatic transmissions should have the idle speed adjusted with the parking brake on and transmission in "drive." *Be careful.* You may wish to have a friend sit in the car with his foot on the brake.
- If idle speed is set too high, the car will tend to creep forward when in gear. Try to avoid this dangerous situation.
- Some cars equipped with air-conditioning must have the idle adjusted with the air-conditioning operating. Check with your dealer or mechanic if you're not sure.

- The idle-mixture screws on some cars have plastic caps, collars, or other devices attached to prevent you from adjusting the mixture. If this is the case, don't attempt to adjust the mixture, but have a competent mechanic do it if you think it is necessary.
- Large, four-barrel carburetors often have two mixture screws. Be sure to adjust both of them.

Replace Ignition Wires

PURPOSE

To provide the best possible delivery of electrical power to the spark plugs.

MATERIALS

Replacement wires for the make and model of your car
Masking tape
Pen

Figs. 51 and 52. With a cold engine, the choke plate should be fully closed (left). The plate should pop open slightly when the engine starts (right). If not, the choke's vacuum control needs adjustment or replacement.

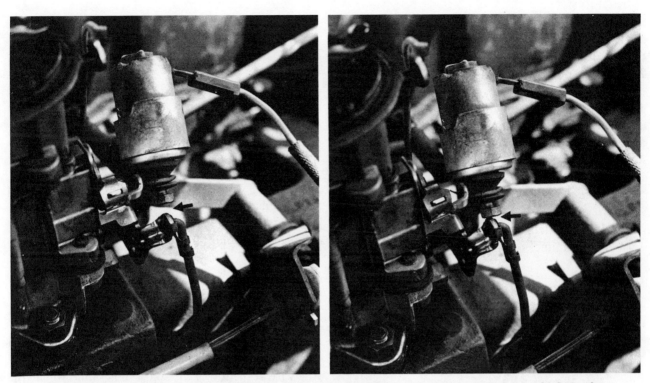

Figs. 53 and 54. Many cars use special anti-dieseling devices, the most common of which is the anti-dieseling solenoid. Solenoids on all cars are essentially the same. With the engine at operating temperature, the solenoid plunger extends against the throttle linkage or throttle-stop screw to maintain the engine idle. The plunger should retract when the ignition is shut off. If it doesn't, and the wire to the solenoid is electrically hot, the solenoid must be replaced.

Fig. 55. Pulling the wire loose with the engine warm and idling will drop the idle speed considerably, and may even stall the engine if the solenoid is properly adjusted. If pulling the wire doesn't affect idle speed, the solenoid needs adjustment.

PROCEDURE

1. Take the new wires out of their package and put them in order by length.
2. Assign a number to each point on the distributor cap and to each spark plug.
3. Remove the wires, labelling each with the number assigned by writing the number on the masking tape and sticking the tape on the wire.
4. Match the wires that have been removed to the new wires by length.
5. Replace the new wires in their assigned positions.
Or
  1. Judge the length of each wire and replace them one at a time.

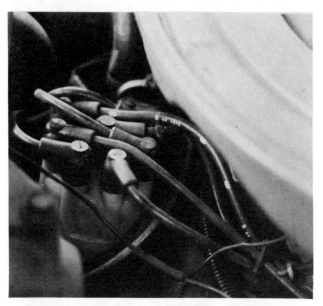

Fig. 56. The distributor cap. When changing the ignition wires, don't confuse them. Take only one wire off at a time, or make sure you mark them properly.

On cars with large engines and a number of power features, the first method mentioned above is probably the best since following the wires to measure length may be difficult. On cars with small engines where the ignition wires are easily accessible, the second method may be easier. *Do not* remove a wire without knowing where it is to be replaced!

Replace Spark Plugs

PURPOSE

Worn-out plugs will rob the engine of power and reduce overall performance considerably.

MATERIALS

Spark plug wrench (make sure you have the correct size wrench)
Spark plug gap gauge
Replacement plugs

PROCEDURE

1. Locate the spark plugs (follow the long black wires leading from the distributor).
2. Remove *one* spark plug wire from a plug. Hold the wire by the "boot"— the rubber collar around the wire at the top of the spark plug—and wiggle the wire away from the plug carefully. *Do not* jerk the wire forcefully. Work on one plug at a time so as not to confuse the wires when you replace them.
3. Slip the spark plug wrench over the top of the plug and secure it tightly. Remove the plug by turning counter-clockwise and exerting reasonable but constant pressure.
4. Some spark plugs, especially on older cars, have separate gaskets. The gasket is a metal ring that fits between the plug and the engine. If your plugs have gaskets, be sure to remove them when you pull the plugs. The replacement plugs you buy will come with new gaskets.
5. Before putting in a new plug, you must make sure the gap between the electrodes is of the proper width. Use a spark plug gauge with wire blades. Fit the proper size blade (check your owner's manual for gap specifications for your car) between the electrodes; it should fit snugly but you shouldn't have to force it in. If the gap isn't correct, *carefully* bend the outside electrode and check the gap again.
6. Insert the new plug by carefully screwing it into the hole *by hand*, making sure it goes in straight so as not to strip the threads. Tighten with the spark plug wrench using reasonable force. *Do not* over-tighten.
7. Continue using the procedure for each plug.

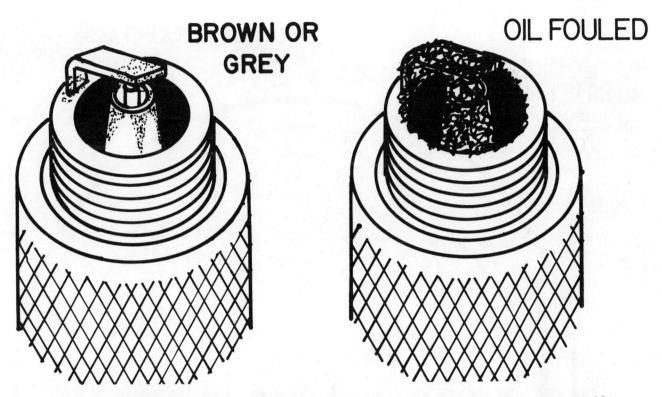

BROWN OR GREY

OIL FOULED

Figs. 57-60. Often you can diagnose a problem by simply examining the spark plugs. (Above left) The typical used plug is lightly crusted with deposits and is light brown to grey in color. (Above right) Oil fouling indicates clogged oil return passages, bad rings, or a clogged PCV valve. (Below left) Carbon-fouled plug indicates rich fuel mixture, retarded timing, or a clogged air cleaner. (Below right) A white or blistered plug could indicate a lean fuel mixture or advanced timing.

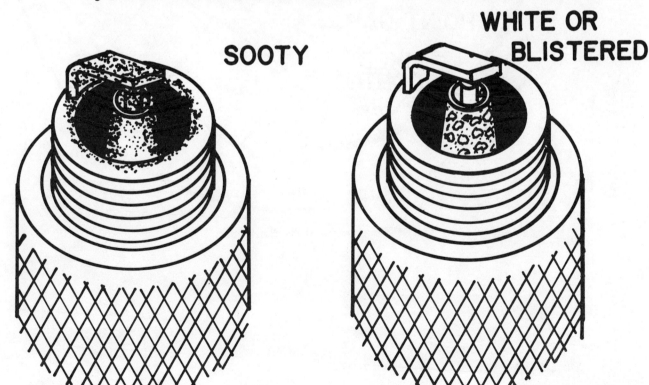

SOOTY

WHITE OR BLISTERED

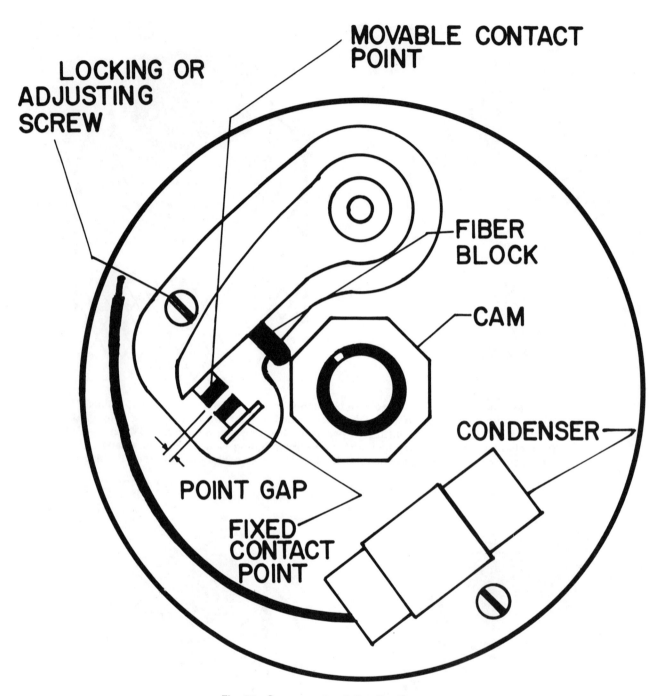

LOCKING OR
ADJUSTING
SCREW

MOVABLE CONTACT
POINT

FIBER
BLOCK

CAM

CONDENSER

POINT GAP

FIXED
CONTACT
POINT

Fig. 61. Components of the distributor.

Replace/Clean Points and Condenser

PURPOSE

To insure the proper contact between the distributor and each of the spark plug wires for best performance.

MATERIALS

Screwdriver
Pliers
File
Replacement parts (if necessary)

Note: If you have an electronic ignition system it's not necessary to perform this procedure since these parts are replaced by the electronic module.

PROCEDURE

1. Locate the distributor.
2. Remove the distributor cap by unscrewing the screws that hold it in place or by unclipping the metal snaps that are attached to the sides of the distributor.
3. Remove the rotor. It's right on top, after the distributor cap is off.
4. Locate the points and the condenser (Fig. 61).
5. Turn the key in the ignition quickly until the points are open at their widest position (Fig. 62). You may need a helper to watch the points while you turn the engine (or vice versa) or you can use a remote starter switch that allows you to turn the engine from under the hood.
6. Check the condition of the points by looking at the face of each. If they're badly pitted or burned they should be replaced. If they're in good condition, simply file them lightly to clean the contact areas.
7. To replace worn-out points, remove the hold-down screws that keep the point assembly in place. Take special notice of where the wires are attached and how they run so that, when you replace them, you'll be able to rewire the points in *exactly* the same manner.
8. Put in the new points and secure. Adjust the gap between the points (again, they must be open as far

Figs. 62-64. To adjust the point gap, the rubbing block must be on a high lobe of the distributor cam (top). With the points held open by the cam, the gap can be adjusted to specifications with a feeler gauge (middle). The gap is then changed by inserting a screwdriver in the special adjustment slot (bottom).

89

as possible) to their recommended distance (see your owner's manual for gap specifications) by sliding the feeler gauge between the points and tightening the adjusting screw. Lift out the feeler gauge, making sure the points are correctly separated.

9. Remove the condenser by unscrewing the bracket holding it in place. Replace it with a new condenser making sure the wire runs to the proper contact.

10. Notice the condition of the rotor. The top of the rotor makes contact with the spark plug wires. Clean off the electrical contacts by lightly filing and wiping with a clean cloth.

11. Replace the rotor by sliding it back onto its shaft (some rotors are secured by screws).

12. Inspect the inside of the distributor cap. If there is any dirt or moisture, wipe it out with a dry cloth. If the metal contacts inside the top of the cap look dull or brown, carefully scrape them clean with the blade of a screwdriver until they're shiny. If the cap has any cracks in it, it needs replacing.

13. Replace the distributor cap by screwing it down or replacing the metal clips.

Timing the Engine

PURPOSE

To adjust the firing of the spark plugs to fit with the new parts used in the process of the tune-up.

MATERIALS

Timing light
Screwdriver or wrench (depending on make and model of your car)

PROCEDURE

1. Hook up the timing light according to manufacturer's instructions.

2. Attach the timing light wire lead to the #1 cylinder spark plug (check your owner's manual).

3. Locate the timing mark on the crankshaft pulley. Mark it with a dab of white paint or chalk.

4. Locate the reference points on the timing gear cover.

5. Determine the number of degrees of spark advance to expect (see owner's manual) and mark the appropriate index mark with the same chalk or paint.

6. Hold the timing light steady on white mark. With engine running, the light acts as a strobe unit and "freezes" the mark in motion.

7. If the timing is correct, the mark on the spinning pulley will be frozen next to the degree of spark advance marked on the timing gear cover.

Fig. 65. Check a manual for the type and location of the timing marks used on your car's engine; this varies greatly. Mark the correct timing lines with white chalk or paint to help make them visible.

8. To change the timing, simply loosen the distributor housing and turn the distributor (turn engine *off*). *Do not* lift the distributor.

9. Keep checking until the timing mark coincides with the reference point.

Don't be frightened by the above procedure. After some practice, you'll find that it's easy to accomplish and that you'll have a smoother running engine that burns less fuel.

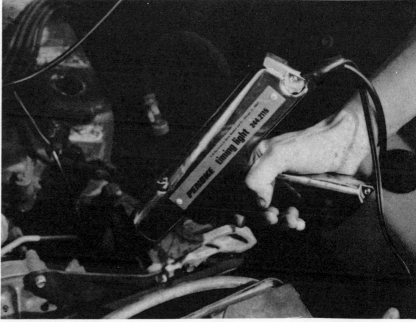

Figs. 66 and 67. Before timing the engine, remove the vacuum advance line at the distributor (arrow, left) and plug it with a golf tee or a vacuum gauge. Then, with the engine idling, aim the timing light carefully at the marks (right), keeping it at about a 45° angle. Aiming the light carelessly is one of the major causes of timing error.

Checking/Adding Automatic Transmission Fluid

PURPOSE

To insure proper lubrication and cooling of the automatic transmission.

MATERIALS

Automatic transmission fluid (check your owner's manual for the right type)
Funnel with tube extension

PROCEDURE

1. Park the car on a level surface. Find the transmission fluid dipstick (normally on the passenger-side rear area of engine compartment—see Fig. 68).
2. With the engine running at normal operating temperature, pull out the dipstick.

3. Wipe the dipstick off with a cloth and reinsert.
4. Pull out the dipstick again and check the level as calibrated on the dipstick.
5. If the fluid level is low, add fluid by using the extended funnel. *Caution:* Do not overfill.

Fig. 68. The automatic transmission dipstick should be checked frequently.

Checking/Adding Power Steering Fluid

PURPOSE

Proper lubrication is essential for the smooth functioning of a power steering system.

MATERIALS

Replacement fluid (automatic transmission fluid)

PROCEDURE

1. Locate the power steering pump at the front of the engine.
2. Bring the engine up to normal operating temperature and shut it off.

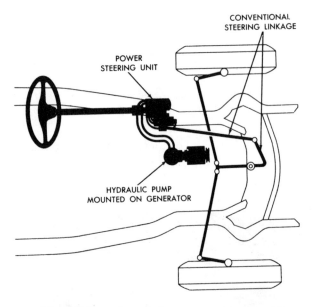

Fig. 69. Location of the power steering unit.

3. Unscrew the cap of the power steering pump—it usually has a dipstick attached.
4. Read the dipstick and add fluid as necessary.

Check/Replace PCV Valve

PURPOSE

To insure proper operation of the valve to prevent oil burning and excess pollution.

MATERIALS

Replacement valve

PROCEDURE

1. Locate the PCV valve (normally located on top of engine head or included at part of the oil filler cap).
2. Pull the plug out of the engine and detach rubber tubing.
3. Shake the valve. If you hear a rattle, the valve is clean and can be re-installed. If there's no noise, replace the valve with a new one.

Appearance Maintenance

PURPOSE

Maintain high trade-in value and keep the esthetic appearance of your car at its best.

MATERIALS

Elbow grease
Wax
Oil squirt can
Spray cleaner
Emery paper

PROCEDURE

■ Keep the car waxed. A good coat of wax will keep salt and dirt from damaging the paint. If you've got a good coat of wax, it will force water to "bead up" on the paint.

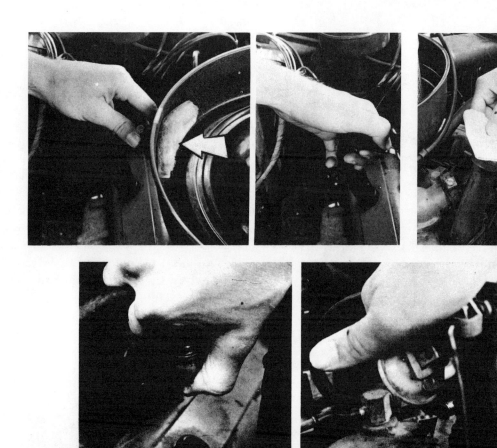

Figs. 70-74. To check a closed PCV system, pull the air supply hose loose at the air cleaner (above left). Be careful not to damage the special filter (arrow) to which it usually attaches. With the engine idling, a slight vacuum at the end of the hose (above center) means the system is operating properly. An absence of vacuum indicates a plugged system. Place a piece of paper on the oil filler tube (above right), with the cap removed. If the paper is not sucked against the tube, with the engine idling, the air hose is plugged or leaking. Clean a plugged hose with PCV solvent and a straightened coat hanger. If the paper still is not sucked against the tube, the PCV valve is probably plugged. Pull the valve loose from its grommet and shake it (below left). If it doesn't click freely, replace it. If the valve clicks, check for vacuum at the end of the valve, with the engine idling. If none, the hose between the valve and carburetor passage is probably plugged. Pull the hose loose from the base of the carburetor (below right, arrow). With the engine idling, suction at the vacuum fitting means the hose is plugged and should be cleaned or replaced. The carburetor vacuum passage will have to be cleaned if there is no suction at the fitting. Cleaning the PCV valve regularly and replacing it yearly are essential to keep the ventilation system at top efficiency.

■ If rust spots develop, rub lightly with emery paper. Paint over spots with small brush and the same color paint. (Paint of the precise color for most cars can be purchased at any auto supply store.) *Do not* let rust get a foothold.

■ Keep the interior clean by using a commercial spray cleaner and vacuum periodically.

■ Use of rubber mats will extend the life of the carpeting.

■ Lubricate all hinges every 6 months as follows:
Hood hinges: heavy oil
Door hinges: heavy oil
Door locks: graphite
Tailgate doors and hatchbacks: heavy oil
Clutch springs (interior): heavy oil

Fig. 75. Rust is your car's worst enemy. When you see spots like these on your car, have the matter taken care of as soon as possible. You may either use steel wool to remove the rust, paint with a primer and a paint which matches the color of your car, or take it to a body shop.

Advanced Maintenance

Once you've developed some confidence, you may feel ready to tackle some more difficult and specialized repairs. Purchasing the proper tools is a necessity and will require an initial investment on your part. Realize, though, that the money you save in repair bills can more than compensate for the outlay.

The following tools are recommended for the advanced troubleshooter:

1. Vacuum gauge
2. Torque wrench
3. Timing light
4. Compression gauge
5. Dwell meter
6. Tachometer
7. Electrical test lamp
8. Grease gun and fittings

As with all your tools, take care of them. Don't leave them in an area where children can play with them. Clean them after each use and store them in a cool, dry area.

ENGINE VACUUM

A healthy engine will create a strong vacuum when the piston is on its downward stroke. This vacuum, if properly measured, can indicate a large number of problems easily and with accuracy.

To measure the vacuum, you need a vacuum gauge. This small, inexpensive item is available at all auto parts stores. When you purchase the gauge, mention the year and model car you're going to use it on. The counter attendant can explain how to attach the gauge and provide you with any special fitting you may need to attach it properly. Follow the directions given by the attendant and any supplied by the manufacturer.

Fig. 76. An inexpensive vacuum gauge is the backyard's most useful diagnostic tool.

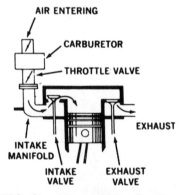

Fig. 77. With the engine idling, the throttle plate is closed and the vacuum is high. When you accelerate, the throttle plate opens, as shown, allowing air to be drawn in, and the vacuum drops.

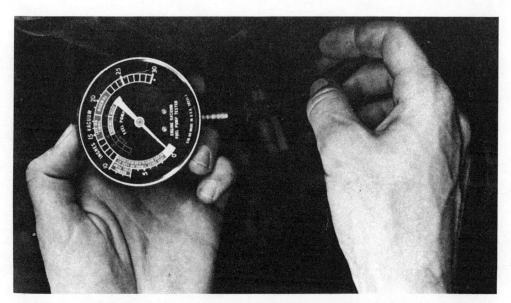

Fig. 78. To get accurate vacuum readings, the gauge must be attached to a primary source of manifold vacuum. The best installation procedure varies from engine to engine, but simply attaching the gauge to the vacuum advance line doesn't work.

Fig. 79.　HOW TO READ THE MANIFOLD VACUUM GAUGE　(See also page 96.)

MANIFOLD LEAK

A very low reading indicates a vacuum leak—probably at the carburetor gasket or intake manifold gasket.

CARBURETOR ADJUSTMENT

If the needle oscillates slowly between 11 and 16 inches, carburetor adjustments are needed.

STICKING VALVES

If the needle drops intermittently, valves are sticking.

BURNT OR LEAKING VALVES

A burnt or leaking valve will cause a consistent drop of the needle each time the bad valve comes into operation.

LEAKING HEAD GASKET

Excessive vibration of the needle at all speeds indicates a leaking head gasket.

CHOKED MUFFLER

A stuck heat riser or restricted exhaust system will cause the needle to drop to zero as engine speed increases.

HOW TO READ THE MANIFOLD VACUUM GAUGE

Reading	Possible Problem	How to Check
Low (below 20), steady	Faulty piston rings	Race the engine—if reading drops to zero, then jumps to 20 or 22, it's a good bet the rings are at fault. Needs professional repair.
Very low (between 10 and 15), steady	Retarded spark	Loosen clamp on distributor and turn distributor against cam rotation. If reading increases, check and/or replace points.
Steady (between 18 and 20), slightly low	Air bleed into intake manifold	Put a small amount of gasoline into an oil can. Squirt some gas at the base of the carburetor. If the vacuum reading varies, gas is leaking into the manifold and the gasket is in need of replacement. *Beware* of fire hazard in performing this test. *BE CAREFUL!*

To read the vacuum gauge, you must attach it properly to the various engine components and observe the action of the needle on the gauge. A normal reading would be a steady needle pointing at the calibration 20 psi.

Use the gauge periodically. Should you discover a steady decrease in the vacuum reading, you've found one of the first tell-tale signs of trouble. The trick is to solve any minor problem before it becomes a major problem. The charts on pages 95 and 96 indicate the possibilities.

USING A COMPRESSION GAUGE

A healthy engine will have the same amount of compression in each cylinder. To test for this, a compression gauge is the instrument to use. You may purchase a compression gauge at any auto supply store. If you own a large car with a V-8 engine, you may need a hose attachment to go along with the gauge.

To test your engine for compression:

1. Run the engine up to normal operating temperature and turn it off.

Reading	Possible Problem	How to Check
Needle does not move.	Valve is holding open on the cylinder being tested.	To solve these problems you will need a shop manual for your year and model car. Or you might prefer to have the work done professionally.
Needle jumps higher with each turn of starter.	Cylinder has sticky valve.	
Uneven readings at different cylinders.	Head gasket leakage at adjacent cylinders.	

2. Loosen all the spark plugs two turns only.

3. Race the engine (this will loosen and blow out any carbon on the spark plugs).

4. Remove all plugs.

5. Open the carburetor throttle valve wide. You may find it necessary to hold the gas pedal down with a brick or piece of wood.

6. Make sure the carburetor choke is wide open.

7. Hold the compression gauge in the spark plug hole of the #1 cylinder. With the ignition off, have someone turn the engine over.

8. Observe the pointer on the gauge. Count the number of "cranks" it takes to bring the needle to its highest reading.

9. Record the reading and repeat the steps for each of the remaining cylinders.

If your engine's in good condition, the highest reading on all the cylinders should be within 25% of the lowest reading. For example, if the highest reading is 160 psi, the lowest should be 120 psi. If there are great variations in the readings, there's something seriously wrong and tuning the car will not effect or repair the problem.

The above chart will help you pinpoint the troubles indicated by the compression gauge.

Chapter Four

HOW TO AVOID
HIGHWAY ROBBERY

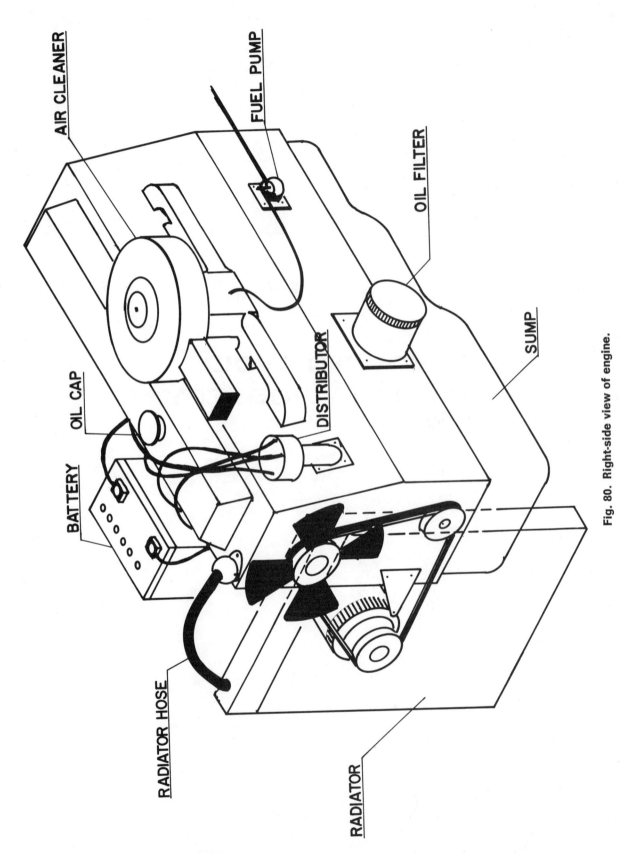

AIR CLEANER

FUEL PUMP

OIL FILTER

OIL CAP

DISTRIBUTOR

SUMP

BATTERY

RADIATOR HOSE

RADIATOR

Fig. 80. Right-side view of engine.

JUNKYARDING

The ecologists tell us that we need to recycle our natural resources. We're presently reusing newsprint, aluminum, glass, old engine oil, etc., but how many people know about recycling used auto parts?

A number of people are aware that they can obtain parts for their cars at junkyards. (Let's clean up the name—Auto Parts Recycling Centers—A.P.R.C.'s, if you will.) If the owner of the A.P.R.C. is conscientious and knowledgeable about his products, he'll be able to provide a service that can save you a good deal of money. But before you go racing off to the nearest A.P.R.C., be advised of the following.

When you go to the yard, make sure you know exactly what's wrong with your car. For example, if the car doesn't start, don't automatically conclude that there's something wrong with the starter. It may be any one of a number of other problems, including the solenoid, battery, battery cables or others. If you question whether or not a part is beyond repair, it's best to have it tested. Bring it with you to the A.P.R.C. and ask the attendant to test it. Many parts may be tested easily and at little or no expense.

When you do determine the need for a new part, ask the man if you must trade in your old part. Most A.P.R.C. dealers demand the old part as part of the deal. They have the expertise to rebuild the old part so that it may provide service for someone else at a low cost. Because of the low overhead and the cost of his product as well as the minimum amount of advertising he has to do, he can sell parts way below what a parts store would demand.

Be sure that you purchase a part that fits your car. Ask to have the part from your car and the new part compared in your presence. Note any differences in the two parts, especially in the area of mounting bolts, screws, etc. Have the part compared and cross-referenced in the various trade manuals at the disposal of the dealer. If the two parts don't match, make sure you get your original part returned to you. To insure this, simply mark your old part with a dab of paint or a scratch before going to the yard.

The A.P.R.C. is not a retail store and does not have marked or fixed prices on items. It may be to your advantage to haggle over price. To your surprise, the price might come down. There's also a high degree of competition in this field. One method that I use successfully is the statement, "I can get that over at Joe's for less." As I say this I begin to turn around. If I get no response, I can always turn completely around and take the part as offered.

The A.P.R.C. differs from a retail store in another way: there is no set inventory in stock. In many cases, especially with parts that are hard to obtain, you may have to call several yards before you find the one you need. Use the telephone to save time.

Don't be afraid to ask for a guarantee on the part you're purchasing. If the dealer is willing to sell you the part, he should be able to guarantee its operation. Remember, though, that you're buying a part that has been used. It may not last as long as a new part, or it may function better since it has "seated."

Another advantage to visiting an A.P.R.C. is that you can learn a great deal by observing the bodies and engines in their various stages of construction (or destruction). Ask questions! The mystery of connecting rods can be explained to you if you have the visual aid of an actual engine in which you can see how the parts operate.

You may also meet people who are more experienced in working on cars. A rule I maintain is, if someone goes out of his way to help me understand something, I make sure that I go out of my way to aid someone else who needs help. There seems to be an informal atmosphere of comeraderie among customers of A.P.R.C.'s. The more knowledge we share with each other, the better.

One service offered by many A.P.R.C.'s is the sale and installation of used engines. If your engine has seen its last miles and you can't afford a new or used car, it may be to your advantage to consider replacing the engine. There are a number of factors to consider in making this decision. Allow the following to be a guide in making your choice:

■ How valuable and in what condition is the body of your car? If it's rusting and falling apart, you may find a new engine to be a waste of your money—it's possible that the engine will outlast the body of the car.

■ Is the suspension in good condition? Does the car take bumps easily? Does it corner properly? If you can't make this decision or you can't determine the condition of the body, ask an independent party. It may be well worth the small fee it costs to ask a local serviceman for his opinion. The A.P.R.C. operator may tell you anything just to sell you an engine.

■ Are you pleased with the interior of the car? You may opt to get rid of the car if the seats are torn or the rugs worn through. Be acutely aware of rust or holes in the floorboard that would enable exhaust fumes to reach the passenger compartment.

■ What's the mileage on the engine you're purchasing? If the dealer can't give you the approximate mileage or is very vague, it may be best to stay away from that particular engine. Don't trade in an engine with low mileage for one with even more mileage.

■ If possible, select your used engine while it's still in the original body. Inspect the body as if you were buying it as a used car, disregarding the major damage from the accident that sent the car to the yard in the first place. By noticing wear and tear on the interior, other dents and damage, and oil stickers (often put on by servicemen when they change the oil) on the doors, you may be able to get an idea of how the car was treated by its previous owner. Ask for the name of the previous owner and give him a phone call and explain your situation. Ask how the engine was running and what major problems it presented before its untimely retirement.

■ Needless to say, only purchase an engine that has not been damaged as a result of a major accident. Usually, rear-end collisions and side-impact collisions offer the best used engines.

■ Demand to see the engine bench-tested before purchasing. This test includes starting the engine and checking various vital signs. Check for tapping valves, black exhaust smoke and the sound of metal-on-metal impact. Buy the engine as if you were buying a used car in a lot. You're better off than a used car shopper because you only have to concentrate on the performance of the engine.

■ Ask for vacuum and compression tests in your presence. Realize the engine isn't going to be perfect, but there's nothing to keep you from getting as close to perfect as you can. Be a hard-nosed, determined, knowledgeable shopper.

■ *Demand a guarantee*—especially if the engine is installed where you purchase it. It's not necessarily wise to buy an engine one place and have it installed in another. You'll wind up with a guarantee for the engine and a guarantee for the installation. Of course, if something goes wrong, each person will blame the other and you'll wind up with nothing. It's better to transact the entire deal with one shop so that everything will be guaranteed. The average guarantee ranges from 30 to 60 days. Always fight for the longest time period and make sure that all new parts and work are included in the guarantee.

■ Once the engine has been installed, test-drive it before paying any balance on your bill. Bring it to another mechanic and have him inspect the engine. If you're satisfied, pay the bill and realize that you've saved money. If you find anything wrong, demand to have it fixed before paying anything. Both you and the dealer have an investment—and you own the title to the car. It would be much more economical for the dealer to fix the problem than to remove the engine.

■ In dealing with an A.P.R.C. you can save money. As with anything else, the old adage, "let the buyer beware," stands as truth. By being aware of the above points you'll become a more aware buyer.

Tricks of the Trade

Just about everyone has a horror story to tell about trying to get a car fixed. A number of newspaper reporters have rigged cars with minor defects and then had them serviced by repair shops to see the results. Many times the minor repairs were made at a modest cost, but also it was found that people were being charged for the replacement of parts that weren't defective, for work that was never performed or for their old parts simply being removed, cleaned and repainted. It's also alarming to hear about people who had their cars fixed for one problem and then found something even more costly damaged as a result of some mechanic's incompetence. Unfortunately, there's often very little that you can do to avoid some of this, but you can at least be aware of some of the major pitfalls and be alert.

If you're traveling far from home, you may be easy prey for an unscrupulous mechanic. Women, especially those traveling with small children, are also prime targets for these rip-off artists. Let's take a look at the sort of trouble you can run into.

You pull into a gas station and the friendly attendant asks if you would like your oil checked. You say that would be nice and he opens the hood. Several seconds later, there's smoke coming from your engine and he informs you that your alternator just burned out. What would you do? Buy the one he just happens to have in his shop?

It's very possible that the attendant squirted some meat curative (titanium tetrachloride), barbecue sauce or old engine oil on the alternator to cause it to smoke. He created the evidence to convince you that there's a problem—the smoke. If you believe him without putting up a fuss, you've just bought yourself a new alternator and he'll clean up your still-workable alternator and sell it to the next unsuspecting victim who drives into his station.

To avoid this, *never* open your hood in a strange gas station. You should know by now how to check your car's vital fluids, so keep your hood down and avoid this type of rip-off. Also realize that if the alternator burns out, the smoke will not smell like burning tomato sauce, but like an electrical fire since it is an electrical component. If the car starts, go to another station and have the problem checked. If you want the oil checked, get out of your car and look over the shoulder of the attendant. He probably won't try any shenanigans with you right there.

Another trick that makes a lot of money for fraudulent stations is to have the attendant loosen a battery cable, especially if the battery looks as if it hasn't been maintained properly. If there's a lot of corrosion on and around the battery terminal, a simple pry with a screwdriver will loosen the cable enough so that your car won't start. If this happens to you, you may end up purchasing a new battery—plus paying for installation and myriad other parts that the mechanic will swear you'll need if you want your car to start. To avoid this, follow the rule stated earlier and always keep your battery in excellent condition.

Some attendants carry a small razor blade to slice a fan belt or two now and then. They don't slice it all the way through, but just enough to allow you to go a few miles down the road before the belt fails completely. As you sit on the side of the road, the same mechanic "just happens" to pass by in his tow truck. He offers to tow you back to his shop to have the belt replaced. Of course he was on his way to attend to another matter, but since you're willing to pay a little extra, he'll take care of your problem immediately. Remember that fan belts do not snap —they fray; anything that looks like a clean cut is very suspicious. For this reason, always carry an extra fan belt that fits your car and an emergency tool kit so that you can replace the belt yourself.

Another "tool of the trade" is a small screwdriver sharpened to a needle point. As the attendant leans over your bumper, the sharp point of the screwdriver pierces your radiator hose and steam billows into the air—if you allow it, you'll probably have to purchase a new hose and pay for installation right there. As you wait for your car to be serviced, the friendly mechanic points out the local diner or coffee shop and suggests that you walk over and relax. While you're gone and the car is in the garage, a number of events can take place, all of which will cost you money. When you return, the mechanic points out any number of things he was able to notice while he was replacing the hose.

Everyone knows that antacids used for indigestion neutralize acid. What will prevent an attendant from dropping a crushed tablet into your battery while he's supposedly checking the fluid level? The acid in the battery becomes neutralized and your battery becomes worthless. What will prevent an attendant from not pushing the oil dipstick all the way into the crankcase, thus showing a low oil-level reading? Nothing, unless you're on the lookout for it. What will prevent the same attendant from "pouring" an empty can of oil into your engine and charging you for it? He'll then shove the dipstick all the way in and dutifully show you that your level is where it should be.

All the above problems can happen when you open your car's hood to the unscrupulous mechanic. The best way to avoid these tactics is to check the fluids yourself. By doing so, you avoid the problems altogether. Also get into the habit of getting out of your car when at the gas pumps. There may be some tricks yet to be discovered! Be careful and remember that you have a large amount of money invested in your automobile and to spend more than necessary is wasteful.

If you do find a "sudden malfunction," all is still not lost. Remember to carry a basic emergency kit and tools to fix the problem yourself. Or you can temporarily patch up the problem (as with the use of duct tape for a leaky radiator hose) until you can get home or to a mechanic you can trust. Whenever you feel that a salesman/mechanic is trying to sell you a needless part, ask him for his name and address. This will throw some doubt into his mind and, if he's reluctant to give you his name and address, you may find that your suspicions are well founded.

Rip-off artists have other ways of getting your money without poking under the hood. You pull into the station, and before you know it, the attendant is on his hands and knees looking under your car. He then informs you that your shock absorber is leaking fluid or that your engine is leaking oil. What he may have done is to squirt, with a concealed oil can, some old engine oil under the parts of the car that he now says are leaking. What would you do? Buy four shocks? Have a new oil pan gasket installed?

The way to avoid this scam is to observe the ground around the pumps. If there's an inordinate number of oil stains present, this tactic may have been used quite often by the attendant. Check your own oil. Also realize that shock absorbers rarely, if ever, leak from the bottom. Take a good look at your shocks. If they're not leaking from the top, you

may be the next intended victim of this particular attendant.

Due to their high mark-up and importance, tire-replacing has become one of the big scams in the fraudulent repair industry. You pull into a station and the smiling attendant asks if you'd like your tire pressure checked. When he goes to the rear passenger-side tire, he lets out some air, slashes the valve with a razor, or punctures the tire. After filling your gas tank he warns you that the tire he just put air in has lost a great deal of pressure. You ask him to check it out and he does. You can request that your spare be placed on your car, but in the process of putting on the spare it goes flat too. You now are the proud owner of *two* new tires purchased at a (pardon the pun) inflated price. As you leave, the mechanic plugs the holes in your old tires and sells them to the next sucker who drives in.

Again, the best way to avoid all this is simply to be aware of what can happen. Check the pressure on your own tires or look over the shoulder of the attendant as he checks it. You can demand your old tire(s) be returned to you and you can have them inspected later by someone you trust. Proving that the attendant damaged the tire purposely will be difficult, though.

Let's say you bring your car to a service station to be evaluated for a problem that you can't diagnose. What can happen? The following strategies are used all too often to take customers for millions of dollars each year:

■ The mechanic can charge you for more time than it actually took to fix your car. There's really very little you can do in this case unless you stay at the repair shop and watch your car being worked on. Even then, you'll probably be told that you must sit in the customer waiting room for "insurance reasons." One time I brought my car into a dealer for a tune-up and a 24,000-mile maintenance check. To keep my warranty in effect, this had to be done by the dealer.

I arrived at 3:30 P.M. and had to sit in the waiting room. The mechanic who was working on my car left work at 4:00 P.M. without informing the supervisor that he wasn't finished with my car. At 8.00 P.M. I finally bullied my way into the shop to find that my car had not been touched since 4:00 P.M. At 9:30 P.M. I was informed that my car was fin-

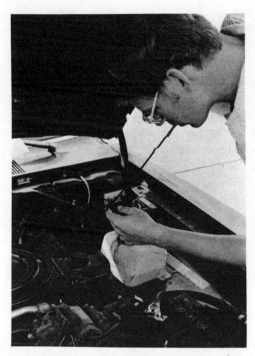

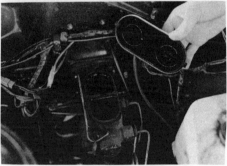

Figs. 81-83. Always check your car's fluids before leaving on a long trip and when traveling. It will make you less vulnerable to unscrupulous mechanics.

ished, and the labor charge read 6 hours. I had to argue for over an hour before I finally convinced the manager what happened.

The next day my air-conditioner didn't work. I called the dealer and was told that it needed a charge of coolant. Upon looking at the appliance, I found two wires not connected. When I connected them, the conditioner worked fine. You don't think they would have asked me to pay for the coolant instead of putting the wires back together, do you? Never!

To avoid being overcharged on time, you can demand that you be charged the flat-rate schedule for the repair you're having done. Usually a good mechanic can work faster than the manual says it should take him to perform that particular job, but at least you won't be excessively overcharged. If you feel there's an excessive overcharge, demand to see the flat-rate schedule. It'll put some meat in your argument.

▪ I wonder how many of you have received the "strategic phone call" from a mechanic. This call is usually placed an hour or two after you've dropped

off your car and usually informs you that something else has been found wrong with your car and asks if you want it fixed since the car is already in the shop. You obviously aren't in a good position to make an educated decision and, if the car isn't fixed right away, you may find yourself hung up for transportation. Reluctantly you tell the mechanic to go ahead and fix whatever he says is wrong. That's your mistake. The best position to take is to tell the mechanic to wait, that you'll stop by to see the problem later. Always make sure there's a real need for a repair before blindly allowing one to take place.

▪ Another interesting technique is known in some circles as "the board meeting." In this instance you drive your car into the shop and, even before the hood is raised, the mechanic begins to whistle and a serious look comes over his face. He then calls the other mechanics over and maybe the guy who owns the butcher shop across the street. By the time they finish talking and pointing, you feel like your car has received its last rites. Obviously this can be a well-rehearsed act to make you think you're in need of more expensive repairs than are really necessary. *Do not* fall for the act. Get a second or even a third opinion. And always remember that a mechanic cannot tell you that you need major engine work without performing compression, vacuum, and other diagnostic tests.

■ Most of us use our cars daily. If the car is in the repair shop for a long period of time, we find that it can be a tremendous inconvenience. Many mechanics are aware of this and they realize that you might be willing to pay for any type of repair to get your car back. If this tactic is used on you, do not hesitate to bring your car, even if you have to have it towed, to another shop. You may have to pay for work that has already been completed, but it may be well worth it to get your car back.

■ *Always* demand that the used parts be returned to you. In many cases the parts can be bench-tested to discover whether or not they were in need of replacement. To insure that your parts are returned to you, simply mark them with a dab or two of nail polish. If you can't find your marks on the returned parts, chances are your car has the same parts in it that you drove in with and you have been taken for a ride. If this happens to you, sue—you've got a good case and will help other drivers avoid the same trap. Whenever possible, bring a friend or relative with you so that you'll have a witness as to what has happened.

■ Some shops and franchises of national chains offer some services at very low prices. Always be careful since these "leaders" may be part of a "bait and switch" tactic—you may find yourself being pressured to have a more complicated and expensive repair performed on your car. This extra repair is offered at an inflated price to offset the cost of the low-priced special. To avoid this tactic, demand *only* the special service at the advertised price. Bring a copy of the advertisement with you. If there's the possibility of something being wrong that's not included in the special, go elsewhere.

■ The biggest money-maker in the area of auto repair is the transmission overhaul or replacement. In far too many cases, the need for a major overhaul or replacement is not real—a simple adjustment is

all that's necessary. The transmission shops may figure you to be a one-shot customer since the large majority of car owners seldom replace more than one transmission in the life of a car. With this in mind, they may try to soak you for as much money as possible. The only way to avoid this problem is to make sure you *absolutely* need the transmission work performed before you allow anyone to take your transmission apart. One horror story a friend of mine tells is the one where he took his car in to be looked at and when he received the estimate, he thought it was way out of line. When he refused to have the car fixed at that shop, he was led into the service bay only to find his transmission in hundreds of pieces lying all over the shop. "Fine, sir, now please remove your car so we can work on our other projects." What would you do?

■ Finally, let's look at the guarantee—that wonderful piece of paper that is your security blanket. In many cases, guarantees are only valid if you stop back at the shop for periodic maintenance on the part(s) guaranteed. This is rather silly, since the cost of the periodic maintenance may be more than that of replacing the part in the long run. It also gives the mechanic an opportunity to sell you on more repairs. You may also find a time limit on your guarantee. If you're like many of us, you'll find that the clutch guaranteed for 30 days breaks down on the 31st day. Experienced mechanics can estimate fairly accurately how long a part will last. Also be aware that many shops stipulate that the only place you can have the guarantee honored is the shop where the work was originally done. What's to stop the mechanic from inflating the price of the labor later, since only the part is guaranteed?

What's necessary to help solve this problem is for mechanics to meet the requirements of a national standard before they are permitted to open for business. Some type of licensing, similar to European or Canadian standards, is necessary. Such groups as the Independent Garage Owners of America and the National Congress of Petroleum Retailers have recognized the severity of the problem and have taken steps to establish standards that future members of their respective groups must meet. Unfortunately, these steps are all voluntary at the present time and hold little weight. What is really necessary is state and/or federal legislation to be enacted that will establish standards and require mechanics to meet them. After all, builders need licenses to operate to ensure that the roof they build doesn't fall on your head. Doesn't is stand to reason that the mechanic who puts the next set of brakes on your car also be required to have a license since both activities relate directly to your safety?

To protect yourself when you bring your car to a service station for repairs, follow the checklist below:

- Know the laws of your state and county related to guarantees, written estimates and mechanic's liens (a lien is the law that gives the mechanic the right to keep your car, and maybe sell it, should you fail to pay for the repairs made).

- Be concise in describing your problem. All too often there may be a minor problem, but if you let the mechanic know that you expect a major problem, he may charge you for it.

- Obtain a written estimate describing *all* work to be done. *Cross out* any blank areas on the estimate form so that new information can't be added after you have left.

- Do not sign the authorization to work until you have read everything—*especially* the fine print.

- Write on the estimate that all removed parts will be returned to you after the work is completed.

- Make sure the mechanic signs the estimate, and keep your copy in a safe place.

- Impress upon the mechanic that no other work is to be done unless you authorize it in writing.

- Meet your end of the bargain by bringing your car to the shop and picking it up at the appointed times.

- Look over the parts that have been replaced to make sure they were in need of replacement. Test any parts that seem still to be functional.

- Test-drive your car (with the mechanic along) and observe that the parts that were supposed to be repaired actually were.

- If you're satisfied, consider yourself lucky and pay the bill—by check, since a cancelled check is the best proof that you have paid for the work completed.

- If you're not satisfied, write your objections down and keep a copy. Make sure the mechanic is aware that you will not pay the bill until you are *completely* satisfied.

- If things get so bad that you must follow up with complaints, be sure to use the proper channels and keep all information in writing. The following groups may be of service to you:

Your Local Better Business Bureau

American Bar Association
Consumer Affairs Committee
1255 Cook Avenue
Cleveland, Ohio 44107

Independent Garage Owners of America
3261 West Fullerton Street
Chicago, Illinois 60605

National Automobile Dealers Association
2000 K Street, N.W.
Washington, D.C. 20006

Ralph Nader
Center for Auto Safety
800 National Press Building
Washington, D.C. 20005

Consumers Union of the United States, Inc.
256 Washington Street
Mount Vernon, New York 10550

Federal Trade Commission
Bureau of Consumer Protection
Pennsylvania Avenue at 6th Street, N.W.
Washington, D.C. 20580

National Highway Traffic Safety Administration
Defects Investigation
400 7th Street, S.W.
Washington, D.C. 20591

State Consumer Groups Listed in Your State

County Consumer Groups Listed in Your County

Chapter Five

DRIVING ECONOMICALLY AND SAFELY

Normal Combustion

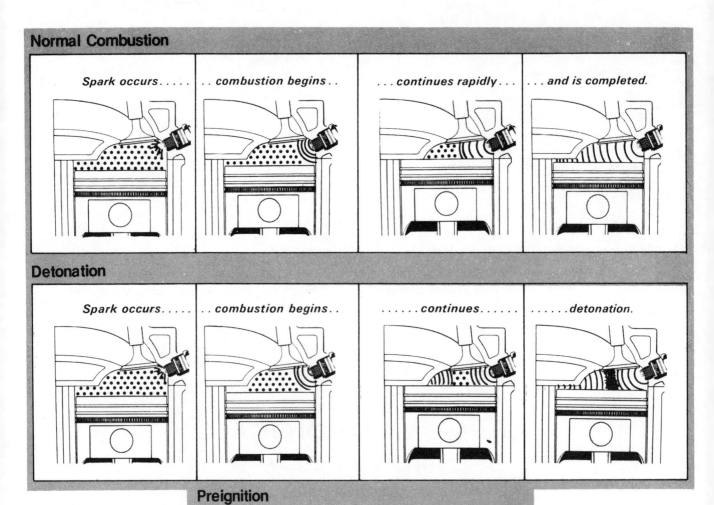

Spark occurs . . . . .   *. . combustion begins . .*   *. . . continues rapidly . . .*   *. . . and is completed.*

Detonation

Spark occurs . . . . . .   *. . combustion begins . .*   *. . . . . . continues . . . . . .*   *. . . . . . detonation.*

Preignition

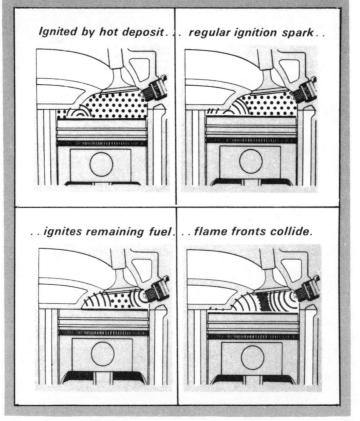

Ignited by hot deposit . . .   *. . regular ignition spark . .*

. . ignites remaining fuel . .   *. . flame fronts collide.*

Fig. 84. Normal combustion, detonation, and preignition.

110

Many automobile owners feel that they really don't need to conserve fuel. Such abstract concepts as balance of trade, inflation and the vulnerability of the country to foreign economic pressures don't affect them directly. Now though, with exorbitant prices being charged for gasoline, these people may begin to see the advantages of intelligent fuel usage.

It's beyond my capabilities to offer a total solution to economic problems, but I can offer some suggestions that might be able to save you some money by reducing the amount of fuel you purchase.

A well-conditioned engine conserves fuel! The following points will help you in making your car as fuel-efficient as possible:

▪ Fouled spark plugs waste fuel. They don't burn all of the fuel delivered, thus the unburned fuel is wasted. Keep your plugs clean and properly gapped.

▪ Old ignition wires don't carry the proper amount of electrical energy to the spark plugs. Change the wires when they become brittle or if the insulation begins to peel. Also make sure your timing is set correctly.

▪ A clogged air filter doesn't allow for the proper mixture of gasoline and air. The carburetor will demand air, but receive gas instead, thus wasting the gasoline. Keep your air filter clean at all times.

▪ A maladjusted carburetor may deliver more gas than necessary. Keep the carburetor adjusted properly.

▪ A sticking choke will cause the engine to "race" longer than it should. If your car doesn't drop to normal idle speed within a reasonable amount of time, clean the choke with a commercial spray cleaner.

▪ A thermostat stuck open will cause the engine to run cold all the time. Newer engines are at their peak performance when they reach proper operating temperature. Replace a defective thermostat.

▪ A fouled fuel filter will deliver gas to the carburetor in spurts. This will cause a waste in fuel, since some of the gas just won't be burned.

Fig. 85. Removed spark plugs should be read for correct burn (see Figs. 57-60, p. 87). New plugs should be gapped to specifications before installation.

▪ Proper lubrication of the engine is necessary to reduce friction. Some oils today are advertised as "fuel efficient oils." These reduce the workload on the engine, causing the engine to require less fuel.

▪ The weight of your car is important. A large car will need more fuel to move it. Maybe a smaller car will be better for you. Also check your trunk. If you're carrying a large amount of unnecessary "junk," you're also paying for the fuel to move it. Clean any excess weight out of the car.

- Always keep *all* tires inflated to the proper pressure. Radial tires improve mileage since they reduce road resistance. You may wish to replace your present set of tires with radials when the time comes to buy new tires.

- Believe it or not, if your car can cut through the air easily, it will get better mileage. Wax your car as often as necessary to keep up its appearance and gain these extra few miles.

The above points will help you make your car as fuel-efficient as possible. Keep them in mind and you'll go farther on less. Furthermore, the regular care and maintenance will also help your car last longer and help prevent major problems and you may find that you'll enjoy your car even more.

The most important element in fuel economy is the driver of the car. In this section, I speak directly to *you*—you can do more than anything else mentioned in conserving fuel. The following points should be considered in your efforts to get better mileage:

- When you start your car, depress the accelerator only once. This should set the automatic choke. Pumping the pedal wastes fuel. If your car has a manual choke, use it only to start the car, not to warm it up.

- In modern cars it's not necessary to wait for the car to warm up. The sooner you get going, the less fuel you'll use. Just remember to take it easy for the first few miles or until the car reaches normal operating temperature.

- Obey speed limits. Optimum mileage is obtained by most cars going around 35 to 40 miles per hour. Speeding wastes fuel and is dangerous. Also, whether you agree with the national 55 mph limit or not, it is still the law.

- Know where you're going. Use maps to find the most direct route to your destination.

- Try to travel during off-peak hours to avoid traffic jams.

- Know the terrain. Traveling over mountains will cost you more in fuel than traveling on flat areas.

- Plan your trips. If you have to go shopping or run errands, try to do all of them in one trip instead of traveling over the same course two or three times a week. Think how much more that loaf of bread costs if you use a gallon of gas to buy it.

- Try to maintain a constant, steady speed. By accelerating and braking, you interrupt the momentum that the car has built up. In most cities, traffic lights are timed to allow for a steady stream of traffic at the speed set by the speed limit. By "jackrabbiting" from light to light, you'll only find yourself sitting at the next light while the guy behind you pulls up slowly. He uses approximately one-third the fuel you do.

- Pretend there's a raw egg between your foot and the gas pedal. Try not to break the egg and you'll find your mileage will increase.

- Look ahead of you and anticipate. Coast up to a red light or stop sign. Every time you use your brakes, except in an emergency, of course, you waste fuel.

- Don't let your car idle when you are standing still more than one minute. You will waste more fuel by idling than you use to start the car again.

- Be aware that the use of power options and air-conditioning reduces the mileage you receive on your car; so does the use of an automatic transmission. These points may be kept in mind when you purchase your next car.

- The most obvious method of saving fuel is simply not to drive when it's not necessary. Walk, jog, bicycle, car pool, take the train, but try to get from point A to point B as easily as possible without driving.

The above tips will help you conserve fuel. You must make a commitment to change your driving habits and put them to use. Good luck!

Driving Safely

Read the following list of recommendations for driving safely. Once you understand them it would be to your advantage, as well as to that of other drivers, to use them in your everyday driving habits.

- Use your seat and shoulder belts. Studies indicate that the use of belts significantly reduces the number of serious injuries suffered by passengers and drivers.

- To avoid whiplash in case of a sudden stop or collision, keep your head restraint in the proper position to squarely catch and support the back of your head. Keeping it too low defeats the purpose of the device.

- Protect your children. Realize your responsibility to your small passengers. They depend on you to take the proper precautions to protect them. Purchase an infant seat with great care, to provide the best possible protection.

When driving at night:

- Realize that visibility is no more than what your headlights provide for you. *Do not* go faster than you should, so as not to exceed your ability to see the road.

- *Do not* "high beam" another car. By doing so you create a situation where neither of you may be able to see. The best method to get the other driver's attention is to switch your lights off and on quickly and let him know that he's bothering you. If he doesn't respond, slow down and watch the right shoulder of the road, avoiding looking at the bright lights, until the other driver has passed by.

- A blind spot is any area around the circumference of your car that you are not able to see from the driver's seat. Always be aware of the blind spot when changing lanes or passing. Realize that other drivers are "in the same boat," so to speak. Do not linger in the other driver's blind spot where he may not see you. Too many accidents are caused by this problem.

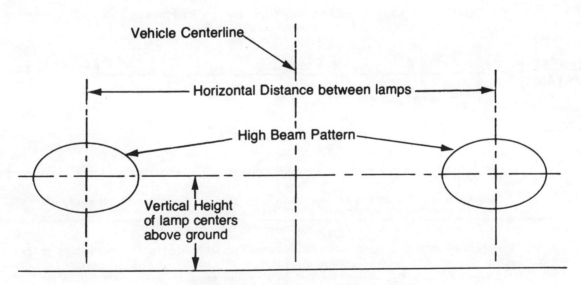

Fig. 86. High-beam aim at 25 feet (7.5 m).

HEAD-ON COLLISION AT 110 MILES PER HOUR

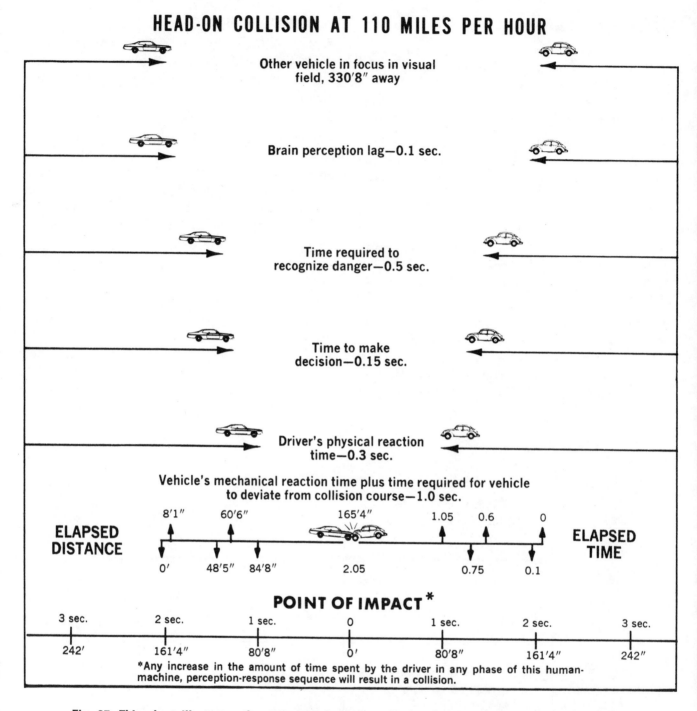

Other vehicle in focus in visual field, 330'8" away

Brain perception lag—0.1 sec.

Time required to recognize danger—0.5 sec.

Time to make decision—0.15 sec.

Driver's physical reaction time—0.3 sec.

Vehicle's mechanical reaction time plus time required for vehicle to deviate from collision course—1.0 sec.

| ELAPSED DISTANCE | | | | | | ELAPSED TIME |

8'1" 60'6" 165'4" 1.05 0.6 0

0' 48'5" 84'8" 2.05 0.75 0.1

POINT OF IMPACT*

| 3 sec. | 2 sec. | 1 sec. | 0 | 1 sec. | 2 sec. | 3 sec. |
| 242' | 161'4" | 80'8" | 0' | 80'8" | 161'4" | 242" |

*Any increase in the amount of time spent by the driver in any phase of this human-machine, perception-response sequence will result in a collision.

Fig. 87. This chart illustrates the estimated human/machine, time/distance relationships of two autos traveling on a head-on collision course at 55 mph, or at a combined closing speed of 110 mph. An elapsed time of 2.05 seconds is the bare minimum available—under perfect conditions for both drivers and machines—to avoid a collision, even though they are more than 100 yards apart when they first see each other.

When driving in fog, snow or rain:

- Always know where the center-line of the road is.

- Realize that high beams are reflected by the water molecules in the air and may blind other drivers.

- The most dangerous conditions during a rain storm occur during the first 4 to 5 minutes of the storm. The oil and grease on the road mix with the water and a slick coating forms. Once the rain has washed this mixture off the road the conditions actually improve.

- Depending on the conditions, realize that during fog, snow and rain the stopping distance for your car has most likely doubled or tripled. To reduce this danger, slow down and allow more distance between you and the car in front of you.

Fig. 88. Is there enough water here for the car to go hydroplaning? The answer depends on the car's speed, the condition of its tires, and the inflation pressure inside them.

- If you should skid, *do not* make any sudden moves that will make you lose even more control. Jab your brakes lightly; *do not* slam them. *Remain calm.* Look for any possible escape or select the escape that will cause the least amount of personal and property damage. It's usually best to turn into the skid and then straighten out after you have regained control. One tactic that I recommend is to practice skidding

in a deserted parking lot after a rainstorm or snow storm. This practice lets you get used to the feeling of skidding so that the surprise you experience when it happens on the road won't be so great that you'll panic.

- Replace windshield wiper blades whenever they begin to streak. Also keep your windshield washer fluid up to capacity. Keep your defroster in proper working condition and, if you don't have one already, consider installing a rear-window defroster.

Periodically give your car a full safety inspection. Whenever anything goes wrong that may affect the safety performance of your car, repair it immediately. Use the following checklist as an inspection guide:

- Make sure your turn signals are working properly. If they're not, it may be because a bulb has burned out. It's a simple chore to replace the bulb (see pages 75-76). The problem may also be a result of a defective flasher. This device is also easily replaced (page 77).

- Check your exhaust system often for leaks.

- Check your tires for proper inflation and for tread wear.

- Check your shock absorbers by pushing your weight down on one corner of the car. If the car "bounces," you may need new shocks.

- Make sure your lights are working properly— both high and low beams.

- Check your brake lights. To do this alone, all you have to do is back up to a building or fence and apply your brakes. By checking your mirrors, you'll be able to see if the brake lights are functioning properly.

- Make sure all of your mirrors are adjusted properly before you move the car. If you don't have a passenger-side mirror, you should get one.

- Before you get into your car, walk around it completely. Check to make sure that there are no little children under or near your car and that there are

Fig. 89. Fog will leave moisture on the car windows—inside and out.

Fig. 90. The condition of the car's windshield wipers can be a matter of life or death.

no obstacles under or near your car that you may run over.

■ Get into the habit of blowing your horn before you back up.

■ Check your wheel alignment by applying your brakes with your hands off the steering wheel. If the car swerves to one side and the tires are properly inflated, have your alignment and/or brakes checked.

■ Keep all your windows clean. In areas where morning frost is a problem, make it a habit to scrape the entire surface of the windows before driving.

■ Always allow for the proper distance between your car and the one in front of you. When driving, use the two-second technique. Pick out a landmark and begin counting when the car in front of you passes it. If you arrive at the same landmark before you've slowly counted to two, you're too close to the car in front of you. When stopping at a traffic light, you should be able to see the tires of the car in front of you—if you can't, you're too close.

■ When stopping in traffic, always keep your wheels pointing straight ahead until it's clear to proceed. If your wheels are turned and you're struck from behind, you might be pushed into an oncoming car.

■ If you have a manual transmission, you can downshift (engaging a *lower* gear while moving) to reduce the speed of the rear wheels as an aid to braking. Once, my brakes failed as I was entering a traffic circle. By downshifting I was able to bring the car to a safe halt. (Constant downshifting, however, will waste fuel and tends to wear the clutch down.)

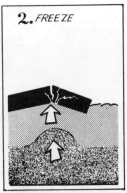
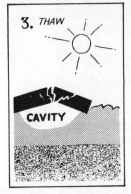
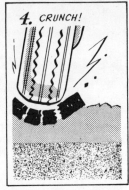

Figs. 91 and 92. What causes potholes (left)? (1) Rain, sleet, or snow works its way into the soil under the pavement. (2) When the temperature drops, the water freezes and expands. This pushes up the soil and pavement. (3) As thawing occurs, the water runs off and the soil recedes, creating a hole under the pavement. (4) A passing vehicle breaks the pavement, causing the familiar hazard shown at right.

As mentioned earlier, the greatest safety factor in your car is *you*. Drive defensively, obey the laws, and always be prepared for the unexpected.

Safety Devices

The publication of Ralph Nader's *Unsafe At Any Speed* made people aware of the safety problems that exist within the realm of driving. Seat belts, shoulder straps, warning buzzers, dual master cylinders, collapsible steering columns, head restraints, shock absorbing bumpers, and other safety devices have become standard on most cars.

The most controversial of all safety devices is the air bag. The air bags work when the car strikes something, or is struck by another car. A big balloon inflates from the area under the dashboard, catching the driver and passengers before they strike the windshield or dashboard. The balloons then quickly deflate to allow the driver and passengers to leave the car to avoid any other danger that may develop as a result of the accident. The controversy surrounding the device relates to the questions of whether or not they will work properly, whether they will inflate when they shouldn't, thereby causing an accident, and the high cost of installing the bags and resetting them after they've been used.

If they work properly, the air bags can obviously save lives and prevent injuries since they work automatically, whereas the use of the seat and shoulder belts depends on the driver and passengers making a conscious effort to employ them. The public will eventually decide what will happen with the use of the air bags, whether it be through consumer agita-

Fig. 93. If this is a familiar sight for you, then you are in the habit of driving too close to the car in front of you—tailgating. See below for one of the possible consequences.

Fig. 94. Only split seconds and fractions of inches separate near-accidents from real ones. Be alert and leave enough room between your car and the car in front so that you have enough time to react to sudden stops.

tion or government regulation. Some manufacturers are offering the air bags as optional equipment on some models, but curiously, they are not selling too many of them.

The safety of small children and infants riding in a car should be of major concern for parents and society in general. Parents often neglect to take the precautionary measures of securing a child or infant properly. Many times I drive along and see small children standing in the front or back seat of a car with no restraints to hold them in case of a sudden stop or collision. Often I see adults holding small infants to their chests as they drive along. They don't realize that the child can be crushed between the dashboard and the weight of the adult should there be a sudden stop or a collision. I see children riding along with lollipops or ice cream sticks in their mouths. Any sudden stop can send the stick or lollipop through the throat causing serious injury.

Infant seats are a must for small children. The seats protect the child not only from a front or rear collision, but a well-designed seat protects the child from side impact as well. If you have children, take note of the possible dangers and take precautions. You owe it to your child. It is my personal opinion that well-designed infant seats should be made mandatory either through state or federal laws, with the parents or driver fined if a child is not protected properly in a moving vehicle.

Again, the greatest safety factor in your car is *you*! If you maintain a properly conditioned car and are aware of the safety of yourself and your passengers, you're doing all that can be done at the moment. Never put off a needed repair that may endanger you or your passengers. Also be aware of the safety factors previously noted when it comes to performing work on your car.

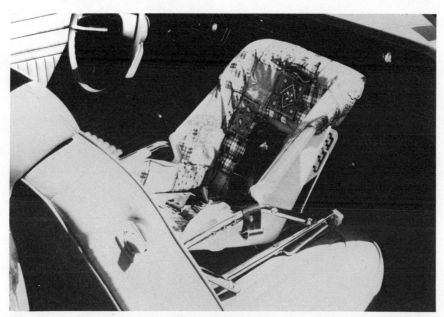

Fig. 95. A well designed infant seat will protect a small child in almost any type of collision.

119

Chapter Six

THE FUTURE?

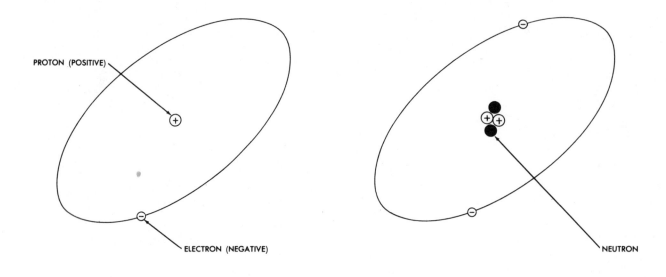

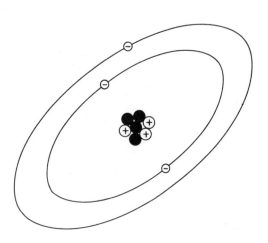
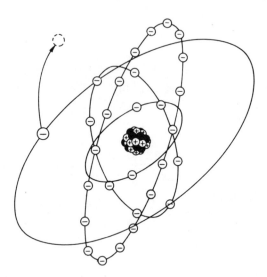

Fig. 96. Atoms of hydrogen (top left), helium (top right), lithium (bottom left), and copper.

The future of the automobile presents a cloudy picture. The major problem lies in what will fuel the cars of the future once the world has depleted its limited supply of fossil fuels.

Recently there has been movement within the automobile industry to equip passenger cars with diesel engines for mass production. There are advantages and disadvantages to buying a diesel-powered car at the moment. Let us take a look at each.

The advantages of the diesel lie in better fuel economy. Diesel engines are significantly more efficient than gasoline engines. Larger cars powered by diesel engines are able to obtain mileage comparable to their smaller gas-powered counterparts. Diesel engines also are able to pull heavier loads with greater ease. Furthermore, the diesel has fewer moving parts so that maintenance may be cheaper in the long run; in fact, diesel engines, with proper care, should last longer.

Disadvantages include the fact that most diesels need to have the oil replaced after 3,000 miles. Also, they do tend to be somewhat noisy, or at least noisier, than gas-powered cars. Diesels are also considered to be slow moving, lacking the immediate acceleration that most drivers have come to expect when they step on the gas. The cost and unavailability of replacement parts can also become a factor for owners.

If you're considering buying a diesel-powered car it might be a good idea to do some research before you make your decision. The emissions of the diesel do not meet the government standards of many states. Find some good books about the diesel and read the most recent magazine publications. Get all the facts before you buy.

There has been much talk of "gasohol," propane, hydrogen and electricity being used to run our engines. Let's take a brief look at each of these fuels and try to determine the status of each in respect to solving our fuel problems.

Gasohol is a mixture of 90 per cent gasoline and 10 per cent alcohol. Part of the interest in this fuel lies in the fact that the alcohol used can become an important market for grain and farm products. The state of Nebraska, in 1975, began to develop gasohol and the results have been impressive.

Gasohol has several noteworthy advantages. Alcohol is a renewable resource—unlike oil, alcohol replaces itself with each new crop harvested by the farmers. The alcohol does not have to come solely from grains either. Ethyl alcohol can be derived from wood and even garbage.

Gasohol can be used without any major modification of existing automobiles. It provides higher octane, improved fuel economy (a disputed fact depending on which test result you read), allows engines to run smoother and cleaner and lowers the amount of hazardous exhaust emissions that enter our atmosphere. Disadvantages include possible vapor locks forming in the fuel lines, hesitation upon acceleration, and stalling. In the test conducted by the state of Nebraska, all of the disadvantages were not considered to be major problems. State-owned automobiles were driven over two million miles (3.2 million km) and it was found that the advantages of using gasohol far outweighed the disadvantages. If gasohol is available in your area, you may wish to try a tankful and see for yourself.

Economically there are some problems with gasohol. At present it costs quite a bit to distill ethyl alcohol, so gasohol is not cheaper to use than gasoline at this moment. Also, in terms of cost, it takes more fossil fuel to produce the alcohol than the end result provides. New technology is needed to reduce this cost and to make the process more efficient.

An alternative source of fuel that's plentiful is propane. To power your car with propane, the car will need its fuel system modified to accept this type of fuel and conversion of an existing gasoline engine can be quite an investment. You'll also need a large car to accommodate the size of the propane cylinder —the propane equipment, even on large model cars, will take up much of the existing trunk space. Other modifications include the building of a firewall between the trunk and the passenger compartment, fuel switching mechanisms and other safety devices.

One of the major advantages of propane is that it offers quite a saving over the per unit cost of gasoline. Another plus for the propane system is the fact that emissions are much less than those produced by gasoline. Engines that use propane as a fuel run better and cleaner, oil life is extended, spark plugs don't develop carbon deposits and octane is increased.

With all of this information, it sounds as if propane is the answer to the energy problem. It would be nice if this were so. Unfortunately the following problems exist with the use of propane as a motor fuel:

- The high initial cost of installation of the fuel system.
- Mileage is decreased about 15 to 20 per cent with the use of propane.
- There just aren't enough propane dealers who have the proper equipment to deliver propane to a motor vehicle safely and accurately at this time.
- Some areas don't allow propane-carrying vehicles to pass through tunnels or over bridges. Taking the detours or avoiding these areas can be both time-consuming and expensive. The fine for violating the restrictions is usually quite high.
- Trunk space is reduced dramatically.
- The propane tank cannot be "filled up" since room must be left for the expansion of the gas during temperature changes.

If you feel that you'd like to convert your car to use propane, or at least investigate the possibility, there are a number of dealers who install such systems. Use the yellow pages of the telephone book under "Gas — Liquefied Petroleum." The government of New Zealand has taken the lead in promoting propane as a fuel for commercial vehicles. The main concept in New Zealand is to make more gasoline available for private automobiles.

The use of hydrogen to power automobiles is another possibility that holds promise. The advantages of hydrogen as a fuel are threefold. First of all, hydrogen is the most abundant element in the universe. Two-thirds of all the atoms that make up water are

hydrogen atoms. Indeed, separating water to obtain hydrogen may be the simplest way to obtain this fuel, and we've certainly got a lot more water than oil on our planet.

Hydrogen also yields a great deal more energy than gasoline. Furthermore, the main waste product of hydrogen is water vapor—a product that is obviously less harmful than the pollutants that are the by-products of gasoline combustion.

Why, then, aren't we using hydrogen power for transportation? Well, the main problem lies in keeping the fuel contained. Hydrogen gas is very difficult to store—it usually requires very low temperatures, very high pressures, or both. Work is being done, though, with metal hydrides — solid substances which, when properly treated, release hydrogen gas. This technology, however, is not ready to be marketed.

The future does hold another promise, although it seems somewhat tentative at the moment. This promise lies in the development of electrically powered cars.

The major advantage of electric cars is the fact that they don't use any liquid fuels to directly power the engine. Refueling an electric car will be accomplished overnight at the owner's convenience. The cost of recharging the electric car will be minute compared to the expected cost of gasoline and diesel fuels in the near future. Another advantage of the electric car will be the lack of pollution. Electric cars will dramatically reduce the carbon monoxide and noise pollution that are presently a major part of our urban centers.

There are disadvantages though. The usual range of electric cars at this writing is in the area of 40 to 45 miles (64 to 72 km) per charge. This obviously makes a long trip impractical. New batteries are being developed and tested, though. General Motors recently announced the development of a battery that will provide greater range and is lighter in weight than standard lead/acid batteries. Some types of new battery materials that are being experimented with include lead/lead dioxide, nickel/iron, nickel/zinc, zinc/air, lithium/metal sulfide, sodium/sulfur, zinc/chlorine and others. Research also has to be developed to improve the acceleration and climbing power of the electric car. Different transmissions have been developed that should lick these problems along with the development of the power system.

Once a successful battery has been developed that can recharge easily, has decent range, and enables an automobile to travel at 50 to 60 miles per hour (80-96 km/hr), we may see the gasoline engine replaced on our roads. The projected date for a truly dependable and workable battery seems to be in the area of 1990 to 1995. Hopefully the year 2000 will find the electric car a viable alternative to the gasoline-powered auto.

If you were to attempt to buy an electric car today, you would find that there are a limited number of manufacturers and distributors. Time will tell and the market will dictate whether or not electric car manufacturers and distributors will be common.

The price of the few available electric automobiles is quite high at the moment, compared to the regular gasoline-powered autos. Once the designs have been established and competition begins to develop, there will (we hope) be a drastic reduction in price—costs will diminish for manufacturers once the demand and volume have reached a substantial level to make expansion of facilities worthwhile.

In the meantime, there are some hybrid alternatives that are available. Some run on gasoline or diesel power, but are able to switch to electric power when the traffic conditions warrant. Some developments include the use of regenerative power, such as the use of the braking power of the car, to be recycled into energy to recharge the batteries.

Although the use of electricity is in the future, it seems apparent that we'll someday be commuting to work over short distances by way of electrically-powered vehicles. Maybe your second car will be an electric for use around town.

The most startling development of recent times has been the announcement by Ralph Moody and Mike Shetley. They placed a Perkin's diesel engine (the type of engine that's been used for over 20 years to power irrigation pumps and sailboats) into a late-model new car, redesigned certain components of the car for maximum fuel economy, and turbocharged the engine. There are some secrets, of course, but the end result is a compact car capable of traveling at normal highway speeds and attaining 84.1 miles per gallon (139.6 km/hr) or 1513.8 miles per tankful of (2422 km/tankful) diesel fuel.

The secret to the mileage factor is the use of a turbocharger. The turbocharger has been around for about 20 years. It's basically a turbine powered by the exhaust gases being forced through the exhaust system. The turbine drives a supercharger on the engine. This increases engine power without affecting fuel mileage because almost all (99 per cent) of the fuel is burned; this also reduces the amount of harmful exhausts emitted into the atmosphere. This "Moodymobile" will satisfy any emissions standards.

All is not perfect though. The Moodymobile must pass all the safety requirements and other environmental tests. These are being worked on as you read this and the makers are optimistic that we may soon be able to drive their "re-invention" of the car.

If you wish to obtain more information about it, you may write to Performance Proven Inc., Box 178, Oak Hill, Florida 32757.

INDEX

(Bold face pages refer to glossary definitions; italics refer to maintenance and repair procedures.)

6 60